Using GPS

Third Edition

Bruce Grubbs

FALCONGUIDES

GUILFORD, CONNECTICUT
HELENA, MONTANA

AN IMPRINT OF ROWMAN & LITTLEFIELD

I would like to thank longtime friend Jean Rukkila for a fine job of proofreading the first edition of this book. Thanks to David Legere, Staci Zacharski, and Antoinette Smith, my editors, and the entire fine people at Globe Pequot who have turned my writing and illustration efforts into another book. Moreover, special thanks to Duart Martin, who got me started with GPS and then supported this project through its numerous twists and turns.

FALCONGUIDES®

An imprint of Rowman & Littlefield
Falcon, FalconGuides, and Outfit Your Mind are registered trademarks of Rowman & Littlefield.

Distributed by NATIONAL BOOK NETWORK

Copyright © 2014 by Rowman & Littlefield
A previous edition of this book was published in 1999 by Falcon Publishing, Inc.

TOPO! Explorer maps courtesy of National Geographic Maps (www.natgeomaps.com)
DeLorme maps courtesy of DeLorme Topo USA (www.delorme.com)
Magellan maps courtesy of Magellan (www.magellan.com)
Google maps courtesy of Google Earth (www.earth.google.com)
Photos by Bruce Grubbs unless otherwise noted.

British Library Cataloguing-in-Publication Information available

Library of Congress Cataloging-in-Publication Data available

ISBN 978-0-7627-5081-8 (paperback)

∞™ The paper used in this publication meets the minimum requirements of American National Standard for Information Sciences—Permanence of Paper for Printed Library Materials, ANSI/NISO Z39.48-1992.

The author and Rowman & Littlefield assume no liability for accidents happening to, or injuries sustained by, readers who engage in the activities described in this book.

Contents

Introduction

Traveling in the wilderness, away from roads and civilization, requires skill in backcountry navigation, especially if you plan to travel cross-country without following a trail. Even trail hikers should learn how to navigate, because trail signs are sometimes missing or just plain wrong and trails can disappear through disuse. Paddlers on large lakes, as well as coastal sea kayakers, are always traveling cross-country and must know how to navigate for anything longer than a short paddle along a familiar shore. Hunters nearly always travel cross-country, and as any experienced hunter knows, it is easy to get so wrapped up in the hunt that you fail to keep track of your location. Anglers need to know how to relocate a favorite fishing spot along stream in and out on a lake. Rescue teams and wildland firefighters are often called out in the middle of the night to find their way to a victim or a wildfire whose location is just a dot on a map and a set of coordinates.

By learning wilderness navigation, you are getting back in touch with one of the skills that makes us human.

People have used wilderness navigation skills for thousands of years, because it was a necessary skill for survival—everything was wilderness until the establishment of farms and villages. Hunters had to find game and then find their way back to camp. Plant gatherers had to know where and when edible plants could be found. Everyone had to know where safe camps were located, where water could be found in the desert, and where large rivers could be crossed safely.

The first wilderness navigators kept a mental map of the landmarks in their local area, and found their way by moving from landmark to landmark. Later maps were drawn on animal skins and then on paper, which allowed people to visualize landmarks and navigate in a wider area for the first time.

Maps also allowed wilderness navigators to determine the direction to a landmark. Using the positions of the sun and stars in the sky, and such clues as the slope of the land and the type of vegetation, people developed the skill to find a landmark even when it wasn't visible—obscured by weather, forest, or darkness.

The magnetic compass, invented in China about 200 BC, represented a huge leap forward. Now it was possible to determine direction even when the sky was obscured and there were no other clues. Using dead reckoning, a navigator could keep a log of the direction, time, and speed of travel and calculate their approximate position, even when no landmarks were visible.

When the marine chronometer was invented in the mid-18th century, captains of oceangoing ships could determine their position at sea within a few tens of miles, as long as they could see the sky. This meant that coastlines, islands, and hazards could be mapped with reasonable accuracy and navigators could find their way to a landfall after crossing thousands of miles of ocean with variable currents and winds.

Other inventions such as ADF (Automatic Direction Finding), LORAN (LOng RAnge Navigation), and VOR (VHF Omnirange Radio) made it possible to determine position within a few miles or even a few dozen feet for aircraft or ships carrying the necessary equipment, but only when within range of the navigation transmitters.

Inertial navigation, essentially computerized dead reckoning, was the first tool that allowed a navigator to determine his position within a few miles anywhere on Earth. Submarines could even use inertial navigation while remaining underwater for months at a time. But inertial navigation equipment is expensive and bulky. Plus, the computed position drifts with time, so other navigation methods have to be used to update the inertial system periodically.

Satellites provided a means to develop a very accurate radio navigation system that could be used globally. The first system GPS (Global Positioning System, also known as NavStar) was developed for military use by the US Department of Defense, but the vast possibilities of civilian use were soon recognized. By the time GPS was fully operational in 1996, the United States had committed to making GPS available to all users on the planet without charge or interruption.

Initially, DOD provided a degraded civilian signal that was accurate to about 330 feet, to deny hostile users the full accuracy. But as soon as surveyors and others who needed very accurate positioning developed a means to correct GPS for errors, intentional and otherwise, there was no point in degrading the signal. In 2000, DOD began providing the full accuracy of GPS to all users, and developed battlefield jamming systems to deny the use of GPS to an enemy. As newer GPS satellites are developed and launched, the accuracy of GPS continues to improve.

Now the wilderness navigator can use a low-cost, lightweight hand-held GPS receiver to determine position within a few feet, nearly anywhere on Earth and in all weather. And the navigator can create waypoints (electronic landmarks) anywhere there is accurate mapping and navigate to that landmark without reference to any physical landmarks.

Of course, if there happens to be a deep canyon, mountain ridge, impassable vegetation, or private land between you and that waypoint, GPS can get you in trouble in a hurry. That's why GPS must be used with common sense, experience, and other navigation tools to get you to your destination safely.

The danger of GPS is that people will forget navigation skills that humans have developed over our entire history. This is already happening as wilderness trekkers blindly follow maps and GPS on their smartphones until the battery dies or they lose the data signal—and then realize they have no idea where they are or how to get back to the trailhead. Even urban navigators are falling prey to overdependence on GPS as they drive their cars and trucks down boat ramps into the water, get stuck on dirt roads, try to drive down staircases, and drive off closed bridges into rivers. This is not only a failure of common sense, it also shows a loss of the big picture. To find your way around a city with local knowledge or a street map, you have to keep a mental map of the relationship of streets and landmark buildings, as well as basic directions. To find your way safely and reliably in the wilderness, you need a mental map of natural landmarks, supplemented by paper maps.

In this book, I describe how to use the Global Positioning System (GPS) as a practical land and inland waters navigation tool in the field, using hand-held trail GPS receivers. The emphasis is on GPS as a supplement to, not a replacement for, classic navigational skills, including use of map, compass, and altimeter. Neither GPS nor any other navigation tool is a substitute for common sense or backcountry experience in the type of terrain you'll be navigating. You should travel with more experienced companions and "learn the ropes" before striking out on your own.

I avoid technical terms as much as possible—but jargon and abbreviations do have their uses. For example, it is easier to refer to the direction toward a landmark as a "bearing" than as the "direction toward a landmark." I explain all terms as I use them, and I describe GPS techniques in general terms that apply to any receiver. As you read this book, consult your receiver's manual for specific application of the techniques.

Contact the manufacturers listed in the appendix for up-to-date information on their models. All of the manufacturers have websites where you can browse through complete specifications and usually download equipment manuals. For those who want to go deeper into global positioning, I have included a chapter on advanced GPS and a recommended reading list in the appendix. This information is not necessary to put GPS to practical use in the outdoors.

For information on using a GPS receiver for geocaching, with computer-based mapping tools, and for online trip sharing, refer to my other Globe

Pequot GPS book, *Backpacker Magazine's Using a GPS: Digital Trip Planning, Recording, and Sharing.*

CAUTION: Never use GPS, or any other system, as your sole means of navigation. Outdoor recreation activities are by their very nature potentially hazardous. All participants in such activities must assume responsibility for their own actions and safety. The information contained in this book cannot replace sound judgment and good decision-making skills, which help reduce exposure to risk; nor does the scope of this book allow for the disclosure of all potential hazards and risks involved in outdoor recreation activities. Learn as much as possible about the activities you participate in, prepare for the unexpected, and be cautious. The reward will be a safer and more enjoyable experience.

GPS satellite in orbit 12,000 miles above the earth

Chapter One

What Is GPS?

The Global Positioning System comprises twenty-four active satellites orbit-
ing 12,000 miles above the earth. The satellites' orbits are arranged so that
several satellites are always in view from any point on Earth. Spare satellites
and ground control stations make up the rest of the system. Though the US
Department of Defense developed the system for military use, the government makes GPS available to all users without charge. Consequently, GPS is
used by businesses to track parcel delivery trucks, by individual motorists to
find their way to a specific street address, by ships and aircraft of all sizes, for
precise survey work, timing, and many other uses.

This book focuses on using hand-held trail GPS receivers that are
intended for civilian use and suitable for navigation in the backcountry
and in self-propelled sports. There are many other types of GPS receivers—
large receivers intended to be mounted permanently in vehicles, tiny ones
designed to be embedded in smaller devices, and credit card–size receivers
designed to plug into data-gathering computers. Specialty receivers are made
for marine use, aviation, surveying, the earth sciences, and the military.

As its name implies, GPS allows a user to determine position. As described
in the preface, GPS is unique among the various methods of navigation in that
it can determine position very rapidly with a high degree of accuracy, in any
weather and at any time of day, almost anywhere on our planet. Using radio
signals transmitted by the satellites, a GPS receiver can determine position to
within 33 feet (10 meters) or better. Because the GPS receiver measures position quickly and accurately, it can calculate your direction and rate of travel
based on previous position fixes. It also can tell you the direction to travel to
reach your destination and display this information on the screen as an electronic compass and on a detailed, moving map.

Limitations

Satellite navigation is not a magic wand. Like any tool, it has limitations. A GPS receiver must have a clear view of the sky to receive signals from the satellites. Since GPS uses microwave radio signals that travel in straight lines, like light waves, trees can block the signals, as can high canyon walls. (Clouds, rain, and snow do not interfere with the satellite signals.) Sometimes poor satellite geometry can degrade accuracy or even make it impossible to get a position fix. A GPS receiver is a complex piece of equipment that can fail or be dropped and broken, and its batteries can die. In addition, the receiver is helpful only if its user knows how to operate it properly.

GPS is best used in conjunction with the older navigation tools. The position display on a GPS receiver is a meaningless string of numbers without a map to plot your location. Although you can load detailed topographic maps on many GPS receivers, you should still have a paper map with you, for two reasons. Failure of your GPS receiver would leave you without any map. And a paper map gives you an overview of the surrounding country that you cannot get from the small screen on the GPS.

Knowing the direction to a favorite spot does not help unless you have a compass to point you in that direction. In addition, a sensitive, temperature-compensated barometric altimeter can read altitude more accurately than a hand-held GPS. While many GPS receivers now have built-in magnetic compasses, the compass must be calibrated every time you change batteries or location, and once again, failure of the GPS deprives you of your compass.

How GPS Works

The heart of GPS is precise measurement of time. Each satellite in the system carries several atomic clocks on board. The satellites transmit precisely timed radio signals that are picked up by your GPS receiver. Each signal carries precise timing information, telling the receiver exactly when the signal left the satellite. Using an on-board computer, the receiver measures time in transit—the time required for the radio signal to travel from the satellite to the receiver. The satellites also transmit a navigation signal that gives their exact position. Using this information, your receiver calculates its exact distance from the satellite and places your receiver somewhere on a spherical surface. When your receiver links up with two more satellites and computes its distance from them, the receiver then knows that it is located on the surface of three imaginary spheres. The point at which those spheres intersect is the receiver's position. Acquiring a fourth satellite refines the position calculation so that altitude can be computed.

The GPS satellites in orbit require constant updates that are transmitted from ground control stations. The ground stations continuously track the satellites and calculate updated positions. Corrections are also made for the drift of the atomic clocks. This information is uplinked to the satellites to update the navigation signal. Without this continuous flow of information, the system's accuracy would degrade in a matter of days. The ground stations can also reposition satellites and replace them with orbital spares as necessary.

The DOD constantly launches new satellites, both to replace aging satellites and to improve the capabilities of the GPS system. To avoid dependency on a single system, other spacefaring nations are building satellite navigation systems of their own, including the Russian GLONASS, Chinese BeiDou-2, and European Galileo systems.

As a wilderness navigator, one direct benefit is the increasing accuracy and reliability of satellite navigation. GPS receivers now on the market can receive both GPS and GLONASS signals, doubling the number of satellites the receiver has to work with.

Chapter Two

Navigation Tools

GPS Receivers

A GPS receiver is a sensitive microwave radio receiver combined with a sophisticated computer. Control buttons and a display screen complete the receiver. All of the receivers currently offered by the major GPS manufacturers offer the same basic GPS accuracy and mainly differ in their add-on features, such as mapping capability. This chapter describes features that you should consider when searching for a receiver to use with traditional map and compass.

There are two basic types of GPS receivers—trail and street. Trail GPS receivers are general purpose civilian receivers (as opposed to military) that are available with and without mapping capability. Mapping receivers can display detailed maps, including topographic maps, while basic receivers have only a general basemap.

Street GPS receivers come with detailed street and highway mapping, as well as extensive point-of-interest (POI) data. While street GPS receivers are extremely useful for road navigation in cities and along highways, they are less useful on back roads. Often dirt roads in national forest and other recreation areas are shown incorrectly or not at all, and features such as trailheads and campgrounds are rarely shown. For those reasons, this book does not cover the use of street GPS. Refer to my book *Exploring with GPS*, published by Bright Angel Press, for uses of street GPS.

Size

For backcountry use, you'll generally want the smallest receiver that has the features you need. Fortunately, GPS receivers are getting smaller as the technology improves; even wristwatch-size receivers are now available. Remember, however, that smaller receivers have smaller displays, which may make map and navigation screens harder to read. Examine the screen on a receiver before you buy it, or make sure that you can return any receiver you order through the mail or over the Internet.

Weight

Minimal weight is desirable, as long as battery life is adequate. Batteries make up a considerable portion of the weight of a GPS receiver. Weights range from less than three ounces to more than a pound.

Batteries

Battery life varies from four to twenty-four or more hours of continuous use in hand-held receivers, using two to four AAA- or AA-size alkaline cells. These figures do not sound practical for extended backcountry trips until you realize that typically the receiver is on for only a few minutes per hour. Even a receiver with a four-hour battery life will last for days in the field. Some receivers also have a battery-saving mode that blanks the screen, turns off the backlight, or calculates position updates at longer intervals. Most GPS receivers use alkaline or lithium batteries, and many can use rechargeable NiMH or lithium cells. Lithium cells are lighter than alkaline batteries, last longer, and work better in cold weather. Rechargeable nickel-metal-hydride (NiMH) cells save money, and the best of them last as long per charge as throwaway alkalines.

You'll want an external power connector so you can power the receiver from a vehicle or external power pack. Most trail GPS receivers now use a standard mini-USB connector for both power and data transfer. This is much better than older receivers that use a proprietary power cable.

Waterproofing

Because your GPS receiver will be used in bad weather as well as good, look for some degree of weatherproofing. The best receivers are certified to one of the European standards for water resistance, such as IPX7 (meaning the receiver can be submerged in water up to 1 meter for up to 30 minutes without damage). Remember that water seals deteriorate over time. Sea kayakers and other boaters should put their GPS receiver in a waterproof dry bag designed for use with GPS. These have a clear window as well as attachment points, and provide flotation. (Some GPS receivers will float, while others will not.)

Temperature Limits

All electronic devices have minimum and maximum temperature limits beyond which the device may not function. On GPS receivers, the display may not work in very hot or cold conditions. If you plan to operate in extreme conditions (in deserts in summer or in mountains in winter, for example), make certain that your GPS receiver can handle it. If you plan to use your receiver in cold weather, make sure that you can operate it while wearing gloves. Touch screens in particular can be difficult or impossible to operate with gloves. Battery life is shortened by cold, so you may have to run your receiver from an external battery pack kept warm inside your clothing.

Accuracy

Accuracy is determined by the GPS satellite system, the chipset used in the GPS receiver, and the number of satellites in view and their geometry. Nearly all trail GPS receivers currently on the market have high-sensitivity chipsets with the same accuracy standard of 33 feet horizontally and 49 feet vertically. Often, trail GPS receivers are as accurate as 10 feet horizontally.

Some trail GPS receivers can receive additional satellites, such as the Russian GLONASS system. This improves accuracy because it increases the number of satellites in view.

In addition, many trail GPS receivers can receive Wide Area Augmentation System (WAAS) signals, primarily from the Federal Aviation Administration's satellite system. The FAA WAAS system can increase accuracy to less than 3 feet.

Some receivers have a position averaging feature that works to increase accuracy when you save a waypoint. You must be stationary to use position averaging. This feature averages a series of fixed positions over time to improve accuracy.

For practical field navigation, basic GPS accuracy is more than good enough.

See Chapter 12 for more information on WAAS.

Channels

GPS units receive satellite signals through receiver channels. To have a satellite lock and determine position, a receiver must pick up signals from at least four satellites. Reception of more satellites improves the receiver's accuracy and allows it to better maintain a lock when satellites are temporarily blocked from view. Nearly all current receivers have twelve-channel parallel receivers in which each channel continuously receives a single satellite. Avoid the older multiplexing receivers found on the used market. These receivers use a single receiver channel to scan the satellite signals and are not nearly as reliable when the sky is partially obscured.

Antennas

Current trail GPS receivers are so sensitive that the type of antenna doesn't really matter. Even when used inside a vehicle, mounting the receiver on or near the windshield usually lets the receiver see enough of the sky to maintain a navigation lock. Under special conditions, you may need to use an external GPS antenna—in this case, buy a receiver that has an external antenna connector.

Measurement Units

Most receivers now on the market allow you to set measurement units to either metric, nautical, or English. Nautical units are important if you'll use your GPS on the water, since water navigation uses nautical miles, which are 15 percent longer than a statute mile as used on land.

Coordinate Systems

The GPS receiver displays your position using coordinates—sets of numbers used on maps to accurately specify location. Your receiver must be capable of displaying position with the coordinate system used by your map. All receivers can be set to display the two most common systems, latitude/longitude (lat/long) and Universal Transverse Mercator (UTM), and most can use nearly any coordinate system.

Map Datum

A datum is a model of the earth's surface based on a surveyed network of physical points, used to produce accurate maps and navigation data. Your GPS receiver must be set to use the same datum used to produce your map. If you fail to set the datum correctly, errors of a few hundred yards to many miles can occur. All American-made GPS receivers can be set to use the map datums used in North America, which are North American Datum 1927 (NAD27) and World Geodetic System 1984 (WGS84). If you plan to use your receiver in another country, make sure that the receiver has the appropriate datum. Maps are being converted to the worldwide GPS standard datum, WGS84, but this process will take time.

Memory

The memory in a GPS receiver retains user-defined waypoint, track, route information, and add-on maps. The more memory the receiver has, the more waypoint and route information it can hold. Detailed maps require the most memory—if you plan to upload a lot of maps, get a receiver that can take external memory cards to expand the memory. Micro-SD is the most commonly used add-on memory format. Geocachers (see Chapter 12) will need a lot of memory to store downloaded geocache information.

Most GPS receivers can store a thousand or more waypoints (landmarks) using short, descriptive names made up of six or more characters and numbers, plus an additional comment field. Current receivers can store fifty or more routes, each containing many waypoints. GPS routes are used to plan a GPS trip using multiple waypoints and change of direction, which is the usual case in the field.

Track Logging

The track-logging feature allows you to record your actual route as you travel. The receiver does this by automatically storing position fixes in memory, either at preset time intervals or when you make changes in direction or speed. The length of the track-log record is limited by the amount of memory in the receiver—when the memory is full, the oldest track fixes are erased. Most receivers display your track on their map screen. Track logging is useful for comparing your actual route of travel with your desired route. In addition, many GPS receivers allow you to invert the track log so that you can use it to backtrack to your starting point, as well as save track logs for later reference. With suitable software, most receivers allow you to copy the track log to a computer for mapping and other purposes.

Track logging can be very useful when you're mapping a trail or cross-country route. Since recording a track requires leaving the receiver on continuously, set the receiver to battery-saver mode, if available, and carry plenty of spare batteries. If you're recording a track in a vehicle, run the receiver from vehicle power.

Database

More expensive trail GPS receivers have a built-in points-of-interest (POI) database that houses a list of permanent waypoints. Aviation receivers, for example, usually have databases containing waypoints for airports and navigation aids. Street GPS receivers have databases of urban POIS such as motels, gas stations, restaurants, hospitals, and many more. The advantage for aviation and street users is that you can pick your destination by its name, which is much easier than manually entering the coordinates. POI databases on trail receivers are of limited use in the wilderness since they typically don't contain places of interest to backcountry travelers, such as trailheads and trail junctions.

Map Screen

Nearly all GPS receivers have a map screen. On smaller and cheaper receivers, the map screen may be a simple plot of your position in relation to nearby waypoints. You should be able to set the map screen to north up (so that the top of the screen is always north) and to track up (so that your direction of travel is always toward the top of the screen). You should also be able to zoom in and out, to change the area and detail the plot shows, and to pan the plot to show different areas. Some receivers feature autozoom, which increases the scale of the map screen as you get closer to a waypoint. Usually, map screens allow you to enter a new waypoint from a position marker on the screen or to navigate directly to a position selected from the screen.

Mapping-type trail GPS receivers can display a detailed map, which changes as you move to graphically present your position and direction of travel in relation to surrounding features. Detail shown may include cities, highways, city streets, back roads, rivers, and coastlines. Look for a receiver that allows you to load user maps. There are many sources of free, detailed maps, which are often better than the proprietary maps sold by the GPS manufacturers. Current mapping GPS receivers with an add-on micro-SD memory card are capable of holding 1:24,000 topographic maps for an area the size of several western states. You can also get maps that overlay wilderness and game-unit boundaries. These maps are often more up-to-date than any printed map.

Even the most detailed GPS maps are no substitute for a paper topographic map in the backcountry, but they are very useful for visualizing your position in relation to your immediate surroundings, as well as creating new waypoints by selecting points from the map.

Displays

Almost all hand-held GPS receivers have liquid crystal display (LCD) screens, but these vary in quality and readability. The display uses tiny dots called pixels; the more pixels, the more information that can be displayed. Make sure that navigation information is displayed in large, readable characters. Check that the display is readable in dim light, as well as in bright sunlight; a contrast setting should allow you to adjust the display for different light levels. Most receivers have backlit displays that can be turned off to save batteries.

Controls

Trail GPS receivers are controlled via buttons or a touch screen—some receivers use a combination. Buttons have the advantage of being usable with gloves; they also keep important functions such as marking waypoints and changing screens immediately available with the touch of a button.

Most button-controlled receivers feature four buttons or a four-way rocker button that allows the user to move up, down, right, and left through the main pages. A page on a GPS receiver is a screen of information. All of the most-used navigation and input pages should be readily accessible. You can enter characters and numbers by scrolling through the alphabet with the up and down buttons. Less frequently used functions, such as datum and coordinate settings, are usually on a menu page.

Touchscreens have the advantage of providing a larger display in a lighter unit. Some touchscreens are difficult or impossible to operate with gloves. Common operations such as saving a waypoint sometimes require that several icons be touched. Some touchscreen receivers have programmable physical buttons that can be used to mark waypoints, and turn track logging on and off.

The best way to decide if you like the controls on a receiver is to try it before buying. An important item to check is the method used to turn the power on and off; it should be difficult to do so accidentally. Most receivers have a recessed power switch or button that must be held down to power off the receiver.

Celestial Data

Many GPS receivers will display sunrise and sunset data as well as moon phases, sun azimuth/elevation, and tide information for any waypoint or location, on any date and at any time. This information can be useful for boaters, hunters, anglers, and photographers, as well as hikers.

Simulator Mode

Simulator mode capability allows you to simulate navigation when you are not actually moving or inside a building where the receiver can't pick up satellites. You can manually enter a starting position, heading, and speed. Using the simulator is a great way to learn how to use your receiver, but make certain that the display clearly indicates when the receiver is in simulator mode.

Data Port

A data port allows you to connect the receiver to other devices to send and obtain data. You can connect your receiver to a personal computer to enter and maintain more waypoints and routes than the receiver's memory can hold, and you can use mapping and GPS software. In addition, some GPS receivers will let you copy waypoints and other data to other receivers.

Mini-USB is the standard data and power port on current receivers. Avoid receivers that require a proprietary cable.

Accessories
Most receivers come with a data/power cable but little else. You'll probably find a carrying case useful to protect the receiver and make it possible to mount it on your belt or pack strap. For use in or on a vehicle, you can get car, boat, kayak, motorcycle, and bicycle mounts.

Accuracy Warning System
A critical feature is the warning system that tells you if navigational accuracy is degraded due to poor satellite reception or if there are problems with the receiver itself. Some receivers use icons on the screen as warnings; others beep and display a message.

Customized Screens and Data Fields
Most trail GPS receivers allow you to change the data fields, and some store profiles to allow change between settings for different activities—hiking, hunting, or kayaking, for example.

Magnetic Compass
Most trail GPS receivers have a compass screen that shows directions and the bearing to your destination, but this information is derived from position fixes and doesn't work when you're stopped. Receivers with a magnetic compass, on the other hand, work just like a hand-held compass, determining direction from the earth's magnetic field. This means the compass works when you're stopped, and even when there's no satellite fix. This is a feature worth having, even though you should still carry a hand-held, liquid-filled compass as a backup and to use with maps. The newest GPS receivers have tilt-compensated, three-axis magnetic compasses, which means you don't have to hold the receiver level when using the compass.

The magnetic compass must be calibrated to the earth's magnetic field any time you move a significant distance without turning the GPS on, and when you change batteries. It's very important that you calibrate the compass before depending on it for directions. To do this on most GPS receivers, go to the compass screen, press the menu icon or button, select "calibrate compass," and follow the instructions. Usually calibration consists of slowly turning the receiver about each of its three axes in turn, and just takes a minute.

Barometric Altimeter

Although a trail GPS receiver displays your altitude above sea level, it's less accurate than the horizontal position. The average accuracy is about +/-50 feet. Some trail GPS receivers include barometric altimeters, which, like a hand-held altimeter, measure air pressure to determine altitude to an accuracy of about 10 feet. This increases the accuracy of elevation profiles saved by the receiver as you move.

Another use for the barometric altimeter is monitoring pressure changes over time. Changes in pressure usually precede changes in the weather, so this can be a useful forecasting tool on extended wilderness trips. You can check the barometric pressure in the evening in camp, and again in the morning to see the trend. You can also display a graph of pressure changes. Note that you must set the altimeter to a known elevation as read from a topo map, or known sea level–corrected barometric pressure, for it to be accurately calibrated.

Maps for GPS

A map for GPS navigation must have a coordinate system that allows you to specify locations accurately. The coordinate system is essential to finding your position on the map from the GPS position readout and to determine waypoints to load into the receiver. Avoid any map without lat/long, UTM, or another standard coordinate system—the lack of a coordinate system not only makes it nearly useless for navigation but also implies that the map may not be accurate.

Maps are produced with varying amounts of detail and coverage. Scale is the ratio of distance on the map to distance on the ground and is the most common way of expressing the amount of detail on a map. For example, a scale of 1:5,000,000 means that 1 inch on the map represents 5 million inches—about 80 miles—on the ground. A scale of 1:24,000 means that 1 inch on the map represents 24,000 inches—2,000 feet—on the ground. This means that the 1:24,000 map can show greater detail than the 1:5,000,000 map but it covers less area. A map of the United States at a scale of 1:5,000,000 will comfortably fit on a wall but does not have nearly enough detail for backcountry use. Conversely, the 1:24,000 map shows plenty of detail for land navigation on foot, but it covers a very small area—about 7 by 9 miles.

US Geological Survey (USGS) topographic (topo) maps are the most accurate maps published in the United States. A topographic map uses contour lines to show elevation and the shape of the land. A contour line connects points on a map that have the same elevation. Topo maps come in various scales; the 7.5-minute series is the largest-scale map and has the most detail. These maps cover an area of about 63 square miles at a scale of 1:24,000.

The US Forest Service (USFS) and other land management agencies such as the Bureau of Land Management (BLM) also publish maps useful for backcountry navigation. The most commonly available maps are visitor maps, usually printed at a scale of 1:126,720, or 0.5 inch to the mile. These usually cover a major portion of a national forest or other land management area. Newer visitor maps are topographic, but most of the maps in print are still planimetric; in other words, they do not show elevation. They do show the official agency road network, including road numbers, and are very useful for finding your way to the trailhead. Lat/long is usually the primary coordinate system on these maps. Positions can be measured down to 0.1 mile or so, which is accurate enough to specify the location of a trailhead or road intersection in your GPS receiver.

Some of these agencies also publish wilderness maps, which cover units of the National Wilderness Preservation System. They are especially good for showing trails and trailheads and are usually more up-to-date than USGS maps. Agency wilderness maps are usually topographic but do not have as much terrain detail as the USGS 7.5-minute topo maps.

Several companies produce private recreational maps. These vary in scale and accuracy but often are more up-to-date on roads, trails, and recreational facilities than are government maps.

Grid and Latitude/Longitude Readers

Although not essential for most wilderness navigation, a grid reader makes it easier to determine waypoints on a map. If you are working with Universal Transverse Mercator (UTM) coordinates, it is possible to estimate coordinates without a grid reader, but using a grid reader is easier, faster, and more accurate. Working with latitude and longitude (lat/long) pretty much requires a lat/long reader because of the non-rectangular nature of the lat/long grid. This is another reason that UTM is preferable for working with maps and GPS.

If you use a grid reader, it must be designed for the scale of map you're using. Dedicated grid readers are available for UTM and lat/long for all the common map scales—see the appendix for sources.

Compasses

A liquid-filled orienteering-style compass is essential for wilderness navigation, even if your GPS receiver has a built-in magnetic compass. There's no point in getting a cheap compass—it will fail just when you need it most.

Look for a compass with a clear plastic baseplate and rotating compass bezel marked in cardinal directions and degrees of azimuth. The compass should be liquid-filled—this dampens the needle movement and makes the compass much easier to read. The dampening also protects the needle bearings from damage. The clear plastic baseplate is used to plot bearings and distances on the maps and is much more useful than a separate protractor.

Because compasses point to magnetic north and maps use true north, it is useful to have a compass that can be adjusted for declination (see Chapter 3). There will be a small screw that lets you dial in the declination, essentially converting the compass to a true-north device. Because the amount of declination varies from place to place, you must set the compass before heading to a new area.

Altimeters

An accurate temperature-compensated altimeter measures elevation to 10 feet, which is more accurate than a GPS receiver. Most of the accurate altimeters currently on the market are digital—either a feature of a hand-held weather station instrument, a digital watch, or a trail GPS. Unless you already have an accurate altimeter, the most cost-effective way to get a good one is to get a trail GPS receiver with an altimeter.

Most of the mechanical altimeters are of poor quality. They are not temperature compensated and are accurate to only about 100 feet.

Altimeters are useful for navigation in places where GPS doesn't work well, especially in narrow canyons with a limited view of the sky. You can use your elevation and a detailed topo map to determine your location along a descending canyon bed.

Altimeters are essentially barometers that measure atmospheric pressure; because pressure changes with the weather, an altimeter must be set to a known elevation every few hours during use. You can use GPS and a large-scale topographic map to set your altimeter: Use the GPS to determine your position, then read your elevation from the map. To set your altimeter, always use the elevation from the map, never the GPS readout of elevation.

Chapter Three

Navigation Skills

Although this book is not intended to be a manual on map and compass work (see the Appendix for recommended books), a short review will help lay the groundwork for the GPS chapters to follow.

Working with Map and Compass

Learning to read a map is easier if you orient the map to line up the same way as the surrounding terrain. There are three ways to do this: (1) Use a compass to determine north (see below), and turn the map so that its north agrees with the compass; (2) if you are on a linear feature such as a road or trail, turn the map until the same feature on the map is lined up with it; or (3) if you can see one or more distant, known landmarks, turn the map until your position and the landmark's position on the map are lined up with the real thing. Once your map is oriented, you can relate landmark symbols on the map with actual landmarks in the countryside.

To find directions, you need to know how to use a compass. You will be working with azimuth, which is the direction measured in degrees clockwise from north, which is 0 degrees. East is 90 degrees, south is 180 degrees, and west is 270 degrees. A bearing is the direction in degrees from one position to another.

Both azimuths and bearings can be expressed relative to true north or to magnetic north. True north is the direction of the geographic North Pole, the axis about which the earth spins. Magnetic north is the direction a compass points as the needle aligns itself with the earth's geomagnetic field. The difference between magnetic north and true north is called declination. For example, declination in the continental United States varies between about 25 degrees east in Washington state to about 20 degrees west in Maine. It changes slowly over time because of changes in the earth's magnetic field. Declination is printed on the margins of US Geological Survey (USGS) maps and most other maps that are useful for navigation.

To convert a true bearing to a magnetic bearing, subtract east declination or add west declination. Reverse this procedure to convert from magnetic to true. It is easy to make a mistake in this process, so it is simpler to always work with true bearings because all good maps are printed with true north up. As mentioned above, it is a good idea to get a hand-held compass with a built-in declination offset so that you can work with true north. This eliminates a serious source of confusion in the field. Trail GPS receivers with built-in magnetic compasses should be set to automatically compensate for declination based on your location.

Remember to stay well away from iron or steel objects, such as vehicles, when using any magnetic compass. The larger the mass of metal, the farther you should be from it. For example, you should stand 50 feet from a car or truck and 3 feet from a small object such as a pocketknife. Don't forget about that knife or those car keys in your pocket!

GPS Settings

You should establish a number of settings in your GPS receiver before using it in the field. These settings are usually found under the setup menu. Refer to your GPS receiver's manual for specific instructions.

Simulator Mode

Most GPS receivers have a simulator or demo mode that simulates satellite reception. This is useful for practicing with your GPS in places without a good view of the sky, such as in buildings. But don't try to navigate in simulator mode!

Battery Saver

Battery-saver mode usually works by turning the display off after a few seconds of non-use. You should use battery-saver mode any time you have limited power sources, such as backpack trips where you can't carry an unlimited number of batteries. You can extend the life of your batteries to many days by keeping the receiver off except when checking your position.

Time

A bonus of carrying a GPS receiver is the availability of accurate time. While it is on, the receiver synchronizes its clock with the accurate clocks on the satellites. Known technically as GPS time, the time shown on the receiver is within a few seconds of the world standard time, Universal Time Coordinated (UTC). On most receivers you can set the time display to either 12- or 24-hour format, and display your local time by choosing automatic time zone detection.

Units

Make sure that your receiver is set to the appropriate units of measure for the maps you'll be using. Most receivers can be set to statute, nautical, or metric units. Some receivers allow you to change only the overall unit system. Because statute miles ("mi" or "sm" on your screen) are the standard units of distance on land in the United States, you normally will use statute units for backcountry navigation. (Unqualified references to "miles" always mean statute miles.) Nautical miles ("nm" on your screen) are slightly longer than statute miles and are used primarily for sea and air navigation. If you paddle a sea kayak or sail, you will be using coastal marine charts and will want to set your receiver to nautical miles. Land navigation in most other countries uses kilometers ("km" on your screen), so you will need to set your receiver to metric units if you are abroad.

North Reference

You can set the GPS receiver to use either true north or magnetic north; for land navigation, true north is easier to use since maps are referenced to true north.

Screen Orientation

You also may have several options for setting your screen orientation. Most GPS receivers have options that include north up and track. North up is the most useful for navigating in the field because the screen orientation is always the same.

Datum

Every map that is accurate enough for navigation is based on a datum. A datum is a model of the earth's surface based on a surveyed network of physical points. In North America the most common datum on paper maps is the North American Datum of 1927 (NAD27), which is used on USGS maps, US Forest Service (USFS) maps, and many other government and private maps based on them. Computer maps are mostly based on the WGS84 datum, which is the world standard for GPS. Other regions of the world have their own datums; more than a hundred are in use.

You must set the GPS receiver to the same datum used by your map; otherwise, position errors will result. The receiver always stores positions internally based on World Geodetic Standard 1984 (WGS84) datum and converts positions to the user-selected datum for display. If you select the wrong datum, the displayed position can be off by as much as a mile. Before starting to work with a map, set the correct datum in your receiver. The datum should be printed in the margin of the map. If it is not, it is probably safe to use NAD27 in North America. Your receiver may break NAD27 into separate datums for the continental United States (CONUS), Alaska, Canada, etc. In this case, select NAD27 CONUS if you are in one of the forty-eight continental states. Most recreational maps are based on USGS maps and use NAD27. Aeronautical charts and some newer maps, as well as most digital maps for GPS and computers, use WGS84. Outside North America, there are many local datums; setting the wrong datum may result in large errors.

Coordinate System

You also must set the GPS receiver to the coordinate system used by your map before entering waypoints or plotting GPS positions on the map. Fortunately, there are just two common systems in North America: Universal Transverse Mercator (UTM) and latitude/longitude (lat/long).

Latitude and Longitude

The most common coordinate system is latitude and longitude, which can be used to describe positions anywhere on Earth. Latitude is the distance north or south of the equator measured in degrees from 0 to 90, with 0 at the equator and 90 north at the North Pole. Longitude is the distance east or west of the prime meridian (located in Greenwich, England) measured in degrees. A degree is 1/360 of a circle; in this case, the circle is the circumference of the earth. Latitude and longitude are usually expressed in degrees, minutes, and seconds. A minute is 1/60 of a degree, and a second is 1/60 of a minute.

For example, the airport at Helena, Montana, is located at 46 degrees 36 minutes 24 seconds north latitude, and 111 degrees 58 minutes 54 seconds west longitude. This position is written as N46° 36' 24" W111° 58' 54". Decimal minutes can be used instead of seconds; the same position would then read N46° 36.40' W111° 58.90'. Rarely, decimal degrees will be used, as in N46.6000° W111.9900°. Most GPS receivers can be set to display positions in any of these formats.

Although lat/long is found on nearly all maps that are accurate enough for navigation, it can be difficult to work with. The problem is that one minute of longitude varies from a distance of 1 nautical mile at the equator to zero at the poles, so the distance between longitude reference lines changes on maps of different latitudes. A special lat/long reader can help you make sense

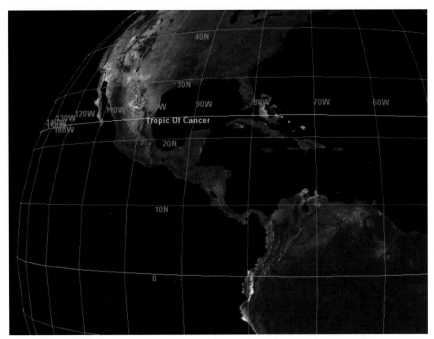

Latitude and longitude

of paper maps; readers are available for common map scales. Computer-based maps are much easier to interpret; you just point and click to get the lat/long coordinates.

Universal Transverse Mercator

Universal Transverse Mercator (UTM) is a far more useful coordinate system for land navigation, and it is becoming the standard for search and rescue teams and others who have to deal with coordinates in the field. UTM uses distances from standard reference points to grid maps into 1,000-meter intervals (1,000 meters = 1 kilometer = 0.62 mile). These squares remain the same at all latitudes covered by the system, so it is easy to read positions on the map. UTM breaks the world into sixty zones, each 6 degrees east to west, and then specifies position in meters north of the equator and east from the prime meridian of the zone. (A meridian is a north-south line of reference.) The position of the prime meridian is defined as 500,000 meters east to start with, so that all coordinates have positive numbers. A zone letter is used to break the zones into 8-degree blocks of latitude but is not necessary to specify position.

For example, to specify the location of the Helena, Montana, airport to the nearest meter (3.3 feet), the coordinates are 12 424802mE 5161726mN. Here "12" is the zone, "424802" is the easting (to the right on your map), and

"5161726" is the northing (to the north on your map). This means that the airport is located 424,802 meters east of the zone 12 reference meridian and 5,161,726 meters north of the equator. You can use any level of precision. If you wanted to specify the location of the Helena airport only to the nearest 1,000 meters, you would drop the last three digits of the easting and northing and write it as 12 424 5161.

UTM does not cover the entire planet; it stops at 84 degrees north and 80 degrees south. (If you are a polar explorer, you can use the Universal Polar Stereographic grid system.) Because the 1,000-meter grids are squares over-laid on the curved surface of the earth, the grid lines are not exactly aligned with true north except at the prime meridian, and the discrepancy can be several degrees. The difference from true north is called grid declination and is printed on the margin of USGS maps. Do not use UTM grid lines as true north reference lines unless you correct for grid declination.

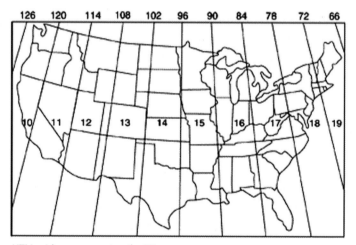

UTM grid zones covering the US

Lat/long and UTM references are included on the margins of USGS maps. Some of these maps are overlaid with a light gray UTM grid in 1,000-meter intervals. Unlike lat/long, the UTM grid does not change with latitude, so it can be used to easily measure positions on the map. A UTM grid reader or any convenient straightedge, such as another map, can be used to measure position down to 10 meters on a large-scale map.

Many other grid systems are used in different parts of the world. For example, topographic maps in Great Britain use the British Grid, and Swiss maps use the Swiss Grid. Both of these systems are metric grids similar to the UTM grid, but they have different origin points. Luckily, the same UTM principles apply to all metric grid systems.

Chapter Four

Defining Locations and Routes

Navigation in the backcountry is all about locations. You'll need to know the location of your vehicle at the trailhead, your destination—whether it's a favorite fishing spot, campsite, or any other place, and many other important locations.

Waypoints

To describe the location of a landmark (such as a trailhead, trail junction, fishing spot, creek crossing, or mountaintop) in terms that a GPS receiver can use, you create a waypoint. (Some GPS manufacturers use the term "landmark" to mean a waypoint, but this book uses "waypoint" throughout.) A waypoint is simply a point on the map that corresponds to a unique location on the ground, one that is useful for navigation.

In GPS navigation, waypoints are specified in terms of coordinates and can be located anywhere. You can create a waypoint in your GPS receiver by

- Reading the coordinates from a map and entering them directly into your receiver
- By specifying the distance and bearing from an existing waypoint
- Marking your current location in the receiver
- On mapping GPS receivers, mark a waypoint by moving the cursor to a location on the map
- Obtaining coordinates from a guide book, website, or friend

Routes

GPS routes are simply a list of waypoints along your desired route of travel. The GPS receiver lets you create several routes, each consisting of several waypoints. Waypoints are used to mark the starting point of the route, trail junctions, turns, and other critical points along the route, and the end of the route. Routes are usually created while planning your trip at home, but can be created in the field.

Preparing Your Maps

Whether you plan to work with Universal Transverse Mercator (UTM) or latitude/longitude (lat/long), it helps to prepare maps at home by drawing a coordinate grid on the map. The grid makes it much easier to determine coordinates accurately. Some US Geological Survey (USGS) topographic maps, as well as many recreation maps, come with UTM or lat/long grids already printed on the map. One major advantage of computer mapping programs such as ExpertGPS (see Appendix) is that you can print custom maps with UTM grids.

Pregridding a USGS Map with UTM Grids

On USGS topographic maps that are not gridded, you'll need to create a UTM grid by connecting the blue tick marks spaced 1,000 meters (1 kilometer) apart and the edge of the map. Use a long ruler and a fine-point pencil or waterproof fine-point marker and draw lightly to avoid hiding any map detail.

Finding a Waypoint with a UTM Grid and UTM Grid Reader

For this example we'll find the UTM coordinates of Aspen Spring on a printout of a portion of the Dane Canyon, Arizona, 7.5-minute USGS topographic map. The printout is 1:24,000 scale, so we'll use a 1:24,000 slot-type grid reader.

Align the bottom scale of the reader on top of the grid line just below Aspen Spring.

1. Move the grid reader sideways while keeping the bottom scale on top of the gridline, until Aspen Spring is centered in the vertical slot.

2. Read 220 meters along the top scale of the UTM grid reader at the nearest 1,000-meter grid line to the west.

3. Append 220 meters to the 1,000-meter grid number of the grid line, which is 482, to get 482220, the easting.

4. Read 340 meters north at Aspen Spring on the slot scale.

5. Append 340 meters to the value of the nearest grid line to the south, 3816, to get a northing of 3816340.

6. Refer to the margin of the map to get UTM Zone 12. The full UTM coordinate for Aspen Spring is 12 482260mE 3816120mN. You do not enter "mE" or "mN" into the receiver; therefore, these coordinates would read 12 S 482260 3816120 on the display. (The "S" is the zone letter, which the receiver calculates from the northing. You do not need to enter it.)

7. Get the datum from that map margin. On most printed USGS maps, the datum is NAD27, but on our map, which was printed from *National Geographic Topo!*, the datum is WGS84. Make sure your GPS receiver is set to WGS84, then enter the waypoint into your receiver and name it ASPEN.

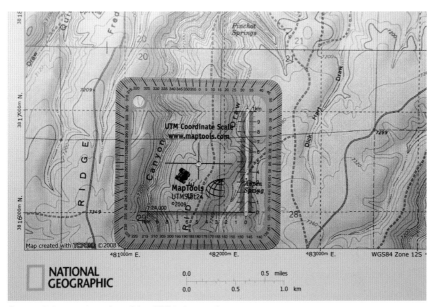

Determining a waypoint with a UTM slot reader

Estimating a Waypoint without a UTM Grid Reader

If you don't have a grid reader for the scale of your map, you can estimate coordinates in the field by using a straightedge (usually another map) to project the desired location to the coordinate ticks on the edge of the map, as described later.

1. Use the edge of another map to draw a short section of grid line from the nearest 1,000-meter tick marks to the south.

2. Use the nearest 1,000-meter tick marks to the west to draw another short section of grid line. (The idea is to define the nearest 1,000-meter corner to the southwest of your waypoint.)

3. Use your straightedge to draw your waypoint to the top or bottom edge of the map. Keep the straightedge parallel to the UTM grid by observing the tick marks on both margins.

4. Measure the distance in meters to the nearest UTM tick mark to the west (left).

5. Use a piece of paper to transfer the distance from the map margin to the kilometer scale on the map margin. Add this figure to the value printed at the tick mark to get the easting.

6. Repeat the procedure using the left and right margins to get the northing.

7. Enter the waypoint into your GPS receiver.

Whatever method you use, read UTM coordinates to the nearest 10 meters when working with a 7.5-minute map so that you can use the full accuracy of your receiver. GPS errors are cumulative, so you want to minimize any source of errors.

Defining a Waypoint from a Known Waypoint

You can also define a new waypoint using distance and direction from a way-point already in the receiver. Using Dane Spring as our known waypoint, we can create a new waypoint at Moonshine Spring. For this example we will use an orienteering compass with a clear baseplate, but you could use a ruler and a protractor.

1. Put one corner of the compass baseplate at Dane Spring, and then align the edge of the baseplate with Moonshine Spring.

2. Turn the compass capsule until the north lines are parallel to a meridian or the neatline. Now you can read the true bearing, 34 degrees, at the lubber line next to the scale on the capsule. (The lubber line is the reference mark on the compass where bearings are read.)

3. Make sure that Dane Spring is at the zero point on the baseplate scale. At Moonshine Spring on the mm scale, read 57 mm.

4. Move the compass to the mileage scale at the bottom of the map, and read 0.85 mile at 57 mm on the baseplate scale.

5. Define the new waypoint in your GPS receiver by entering the name of the reference waypoint, DANESP, and then the distance and direction. Call the new waypoint MOONSHINE.

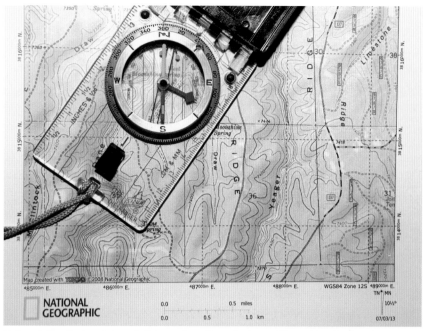

Determining the bearing and distance from Dane Spring to Moonshine Spring

Entering the projected waypoint for Moonshine Spring

In field use, you often can estimate coordinates by estimating the position of a map landmark in relation to the coordinate grid or tick marks. This technique is especially useful in bad weather or when you do not have a UTM grid reader or lat/long scale. It also works well when you know your position via conventional navigation but want to use your GPS receiver to confirm it. You can read the coordinates from the receiver's position screen and estimate their location on your map. Always check a new waypoint for reasonableness by noting its distance and direction from an existing waypoint. Incorrectly entering a digit or two can put a waypoint hundreds or thousands of miles away from its correct location. It is easy to spot an error of this magnitude, but it is harder to catch an error of only a mile or so.

Computer Mapping

Computer mapping uses a GPS receiver and a personal computer to store, manipulate, and present GPS data. Such systems can function as a very accurate moving map and can be used to navigate to street addresses or businesses. Data can be collected in the field and used to map the location of roads or trails easily and accurately. GPS mapping was once the realm of professional users because of the expensive hardware and required software, but several inexpensive GPS mapping products now bring this capability to general users. These products are based on digital USGS topographic data and other map and imagery sources downloaded from the Internet, which allows the software to compute and display exact coordinates and elevations for any position on the computer screen. Once you have experienced the ease of creating, uploading, and downloading waypoints with a computer, it is hard to go back to entering coordinates directly into a GPS unit. See the appendix for a list of companies that produce mapping software, and refer to Chapter 10 for a practical example of using a computer with GPS.

For more information on using a GPS receiver with computer-based mapping tools, for geocaching, and for online trip sharing, refer to my other Globe Pequot GPS book, *Backpacker Magazine's Using a GPS: Digital Trip Planning, Recording, and Sharing.*

Chapter Five

Field Technique

When you use a GPS receiver in a vehicle, run the receiver on the vehicle's power and mount the receiver on the windshield or dashboard. Vehicle power cords and mounts are available from the GPS manufacturer as well as after-market manufacturers—see the appendix. If you are driving, it is safer to have a passenger operate the receiver and do the navigation.

If you are hiking, skiing, paddling, or cycling and run the receiver on its batteries, leave the receiver off unless you need it to find your position or to navigate. Use the battery-saver mode if your receiver has one, and avoid leaving the backlight on continuously. Always carry enough spare batteries to last the trip.

Use all means of navigation at your disposal, not just GPS. On a trail, for example, pay attention to trail signs and use your map to keep track of prominent landmarks. Take notes in a small notebook or on your map as you progress. When hiking cross-country, chart your progress on the map with a pencil. If you save GPS waypoints, write the coordinates or the name of each waypoint on the map or in your notebook.

Determining Your Position

Although current GPS receivers are much better at maintaining a satellite lock than older units, you still want to get the best possible view of the sky from your location. In dense forest, find a clearing or opening in the canopy. Stay away from cliffs—they may reflect the satellite signals and cause false readings. In a vehicle, the receiver can usually see enough satellites through the windshield, but in some cases, you may have to stop and take the receiver outside.

Satellite Status

Most GPS receivers have a status page that tells you how many satellites are visible and how strong their signals are. Some receivers start on the status page, while on other units you have to select it.

The visible satellite display is usually a small map of the sky, with the horizon represented by the outer ring of a circle and the 45-degree elevation above the horizon represented by an inner circle. Each satellite is marked with a unique number, and reversing the display colors indicates the satellites being received. A satellite is considered visible when it is above the masking angle (normally, 10 degrees above the horizon). A separate display gives the signal strength of each satellite by its number.

Satellite Lock

The GPS receiver must receive at least four satellites to calculate your position accurately, which is called having a "satellite lock," or a "fix." Newer receivers typically achieve satellite lock in about fifteen seconds. It will take longer in locations where the sky is partially obscured, or if the receiver hasn't been used for a while.

The position of the satellites is important. GPS position fixes are most accurate when three of the satellites are just above the masking angle, spread evenly along the horizon, and a fourth satellite is directly overhead. GPS positions are least accurate when the four satellites are close together in the sky—a condition called poor satellite geometry. Most receivers provide some indication of the accuracy of the fix. Some use a warning icon to indicate poor satellite geometry; others display a numerical value, such as feet, to indicate the accuracy level.

If you have not used the receiver for several months or have moved several hundred miles since the last use, it may take longer to get a fix. This is because the almanac data showing the approximate positions of the satellites is out of date. The receiver updates this information from the satellite transmissions.

If the sky is partially obstructed, remain stationary while getting the initial fix. If you move around, interruptions in the satellite signals may make the entire almanac or ephemeris message invalid, forcing the GPS receiver to start over.

Once the GPS receiver has enough satellites for a fix, it will show that it has a satellite lock with a satellite icon on the start-up screen, or by showing the satellite status screen. You should always check the satellite status screen to make certain the receiver is locked onto at least four satellites. Check the GPS accuracy as well. With a good satellite lock, the accuracy should be 33 feet or less.

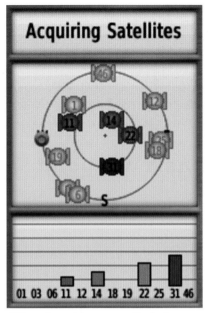

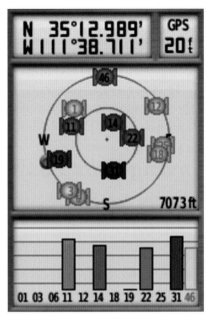

GPS receiver without a satellite lock   GPS receiver with satellite lock

Occasionally you will have problems obtaining a satellite lock. The receiver will warn you on the display, and many receivers also trigger an audible alarm. The usual cause is a poor view of the sky. Because the satellite signals travel strictly by line of sight like visible light, even widely spaced trees can block reception. Deep, narrow canyons are especially difficult spots from which to fix your position. The best locations are open meadows or clearings with low horizons.

If you have to get a fix in forest cover, move around to get the strongest signal strengths on the status page. Once you do have a fix, do not move until you have saved your position or checked the bearing to your next waypoint, especially if there are overhead obstacles. Occasionally you will not be able to get a fix at all. Wait a few minutes; satellite movement may eliminate the problem. Sometimes turning the receiver off and on again will reset it, and it will lock on.

Finding Your Position on a Map

To find your position on a map with coordinates from your GPS receiver, reverse the procedures described earlier for reading coordinates from a map. If possible, cross-check the GPS position with other means of finding your location, such as nearby landmarks, roads, or trail signs. If circumstances make

GPS your only means of navigation (in cases of fog, featureless terrain, or whiteout conditions), take GPS fixes more often and compare them to each other. Never depend on a single, unverified GPS position (or any other single position fix) in a critical situation.

Some newer GPS receivers have a position-averaging feature that improves accuracy by averaging a series of fixes over time. Accuracy of 15 feet or better is claimed. To use this feature, you must be stationary.

Saving Your Position as a Waypoint

You can save your current position as a waypoint any time the receiver has a satellite lock. Most receivers give you the option of naming the waypoint yourself or letting the receiver automatically assign a name. If you choose the latter, the receiver assigns sequential numbers to waypoints as you enter them. Most receivers also stamp waypoints with the date and time, which can help you remember the purpose of a waypoint later. Since it takes time to enter the name of a waypoint into the receiver, it is easier to let the receiver automatically name waypoints saved in the field and take notes on the name and purpose of the waypoint.

The datum and coordinate settings do not matter when you create a waypoint by saving your current position, because the receiver always uses WGS84 to save positions. The receiver converts from WGS84 to the currently selected datum and coordinate systems to display your current position and the location of waypoints. That is why it is critical for you to set the correct datum and coordinate system when plotting coordinates on a map or when reading coordinates from a map for entry into the receiver.

Creating New Waypoints

You can create a new waypoint by entering the coordinates directly into your receiver. You can get coordinates for a new waypoint from your map as described in the last chapter, and from sources such as guidebooks, websites, and friends.

You can also create a new waypoint by entering the distance and bearing from a waypoint that is already in your receiver, as described in detail in the last chapter.

A third method is to create a waypoint from a location on the map screen of your GPS receiver. To do this, pan the map by moving the cursor to the point where you wish to create a waypoint. If the new waypoint is located some distance from your current position, you can speed up this process by

InnerJct
30-JUN-13 9:54

Note

Location
12 S 0439336
UTM   3909541

Elevation | Depth
_____ t | _____ t

View Map

Saving a waypoint

10950 Ft
7.77mi 351°

Kachina Peaks Wilderness

Inner Basin Trail

Weatherford Trail

500ft

Creating a waypoint from the map screen

zooming out, moving the cursor to the general location of the new waypoint, and then zooming in as needed so you can see the exact point to create the waypoint.

Mapping GPS receivers with detailed topo maps make it possible to create waypoints at trail junctions and other features not shown on the general basemaps that come with most units. Using your paper map to find the waypoints and creating them directly from the GPS map screen is easier and less error-prone than reading coordinates from a paper map and typing them into the GPS receiver.

Navigating to a Waypoint

To navigate to a waypoint, use the receiver's GoTo or Find function to select the desired waypoint. On mapping GPS units, you can select the map screen, then pan the map to the desired area and use the cursor to select a point. The receiver creates an internal waypoint at your selected point. In either case, the receiver will immediately start navigating from your present position directly to the chosen waypoint.

The GPS receiver then gives you a choice of several pages of navigation information. The primary pages you'll use while navigating are the map and compass screens.

Note that most GPS receivers allow you to customize the information shown on each screen. Some also have preset "profiles" for activities such as hunting, fishing, and hiking, which allow you to change all the navigation screens to suit your current activity by selecting a profile. Profiles can be individually customized and you can also create and name your own profiles.

The compass screen shows bearing and distance to the next waypoint from your present position, and usually your track and speed. Bearing is the compass azimuth, in degrees, from your present position directly to the waypoint. Heading is the direction you are actually traveling. If you are exactly on course, your track and the bearing to the waypoint will be the same. Of course, if you are driving on a road or hiking a trail, you want to stay on the road or trail. Still, the track information shows whether your current road is taking you in the general direction of your destination. When you reach a crossroads, the bearing tells you which way to turn.

Another item usually shown on the compass screen (if not, you can add it, as explained above) is the estimated time en route (ETE) to the waypoint. Some receivers also show the estimated time of arrival (ETA) at the waypoint. ETE and ETA are computed from the speed you are traveling toward a

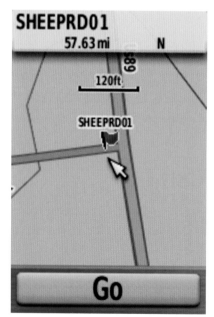

Starting navigation to a waypoint

Compass screen on a GPS receiver

waypoint. This is called velocity made good (VMG). As you travel, following a road or trail or dodging obstacles, you are not always headed directly toward the next waypoint. Thus, your rate of progress toward a waypoint is less than your ground speed (your actual speed across the ground). As your actual track (track made good, or TMG) twists and turns, your VMG and ETA change. Some GPS receivers allow you to average velocity over a short period. If yours does not, you can check the ETA occasionally and average it in your head. This knowledge can be useful in figuring out, for example, whether you will be able to drive to a trailhead before dark. If you were planning to camp at the trailhead but your ETA shows that you will not make it before nightfall, you might want to look for a closer place to camp.

Most GPS receivers have a map screen that shows your position in relation to waypoints. Your course (also called the desired track, or DTK) is shown as a straight line from waypoint to waypoint along your current leg. Your TMG is also shown as you progress. Often, bearing and distance to the next waypoint are shown, along with heading (your current direction of travel) and speed. (Again, these data fields can be added or customized on most receivers.) The map screen gives you an easy-to-understand graphic of your navigation. On most receivers a basemap shows major roads and cities. Mapping GPS receivers can display detailed maps, including topographic maps and land ownership maps. Units that allow you to load custom maps can use free maps from sources such as gpsfiledepot.com, including detailed topo maps.

Although detailed maps are very useful to have on your GPS receiver, they are no substitute for paper maps. The tiny screen on the GPS receiver can't give you the big picture of your surroundings, and the GPS receiver can fail, leaving you without a map.

As you travel, the GPS constantly updates the navigation information. The GPS receiver will display a warning on the screen when you are approaching a waypoint. Most receivers can be set to give an audible warning as well.

At low speeds (under 5 to 10 miles per hour), GPS receivers may not compute speed consistently

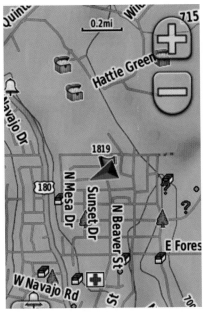

Map screen on a GPS receiver

due to the accuracy limits of the GPS system. If the displayed speed and ETA fluctuate as you move, you have to either average them in your head or ignore them. Some receivers have an averaging function to smooth out the ETA calculation, making them more useful at low speeds. Still, the best way to navigate at walking speeds is to use the receiver while stopped. Get a position fix, save it as a waypoint if necessary, note the bearing and distance to the next waypoint, and then shut off the receiver. Use your compass, the sun, or the lay of the land to determine your direction, and then use landmarks or the compass to maintain that direction as you travel.

A good way to practice navigating to a waypoint is to look for benchmarks and other survey marks in the field. When ground surveys are done, the survey points are precisely located and permanently marked with a monument that usually consists of a brass cap about 3 inches in diameter. The plate is set in a concrete post or rock outcrop. The location of survey marks is shown on USGS topographic maps. Benchmarks are used as reference points for mapping and are shown as a small cross or a triangle labeled with "BM" or "VABM" and an elevation.

Another great way to practice navigation is geocaching. See Chapter 12, as well as my other books, *Exploring with GPS* and *Backpacker Magazine's Using a GPS: Digital Trip Planning, Recording, and Sharing,* for more information.

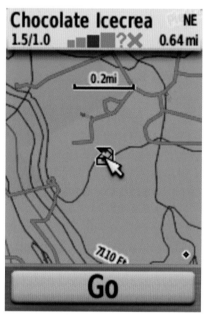

Selecting a geocache from the map screen

Chapter Six

Trail Hiking

Before leaving a trailhead, always save your vehicle's position as a waypoint and name it something unmistakable, such as TRUCK or TRAILH. (Or allow the receiver to automatically name the waypoint, then make a note of the purpose of the waypoint on your map or in a notebook.) That way you will be able to find your way back to your vehicle, even without a map.

It's not always practical to use a GPS receiver as you hike. The receiver must be in a position where its antenna can see the sky, and constant use runs down the batteries more quickly. For situations where you must have the receiver on, such as mapping a trail by recording a track log, put the receiver in battery-saver mode and carry spare batteries. Mount or attach the receiver to a shoulder strap where it can get the best possible view of the sky.

Professional users of GPS in the field, such as land managers and survey-ors, use an external GPS antenna mounted on a mast on their pack, so that the antenna always has a clear view of the sky. Such antennas aren't necessary for recreational use with current GPS units, which have much better receivers than older units and generally keep a satellite lock even with only part of the sky visible.

A more practical approach for backcountry users is to leave the GPS off most of the time, and turn it on momentarily to check your location and prog-ress as needed. This technique also saves batteries. Rest stops are an ideal time; you can get an updated fix and check the bearing and direction to your next waypoint. This is also a good time to cross-check your position on the map using both the GPS fix and landmarks.

On the trail it helps to have predefined waypoints and routes that you set up at home or at camp before the trip. Of course, you can enter new way-points at any time using your map and the methods described earlier or by saving your position as a waypoint. In the field, especially in bad weather, it

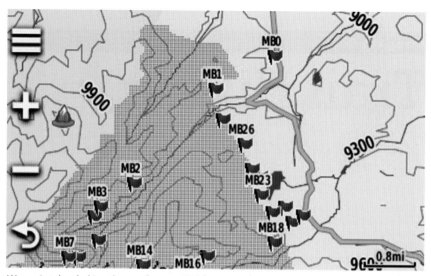

Waypoints loaded in advance for a trail hike

may be easier to define a new waypoint using distance and direction from an existing waypoint.

Even if you do not plan to actively navigate using your GPS receiver, save waypoints at important trail junctions and landmarks such as stream crossings, passes, and campsites. That way you will have additional GPS navigation information to help you find your way back if you lose the trail or become disoriented.

Chapter Seven

Cross-country Hiking

When cross-country hiking, generally you will select the same waypoints you would use without a GPS receiver. For example, you might plan to hike a trail for a few miles, then strike off cross-country to a good fishing lake. In this case, set up waypoints at the trailhead, the point at which you will leave the trail, the lake, and any useful intermediate waypoints. Then create a route using these three waypoints. As you hike, stop when you feel the need and check your progress with the GPS receiver. As you near the point where you will leave the trail, you may want to leave the receiver on so that you do not miss the turnoff. When the receiver detects that you have reached the turnoff, it will automatically navigate to the next waypoint—in this case, the lake.

Handling Detours

Hiking cross-country usually requires you to continually make small detours to avoid obstacles. The classic navigation technique is to pick a distant landmark in the direction you need to go and travel toward it. You should do this as a backup to GPS, but it will not work in dense forest or bad weather where you can't see distant landmarks. The GPS receiver effectively replaces the distant visual landmark with an electronic one. Each time you turn on the receiver, it tells you the direction to your next waypoint from your current position, no matter how much you have deviated from the straight-line course. It also shows you how far off course you are, and in which direction.

Backtracking

The route-reversal feature on most GPS receivers makes backtracking easier. In the example above, reversing the route creates a route from the lake to the trailhead, with an intermediate waypoint at the location where you will rejoin the trail. Most receivers also let you create a route from the automatically stored track data. This function works only if you have left the receiver on continuously.

Triangulation with GPS

Triangulation can be used with the GPS receiver, map, and compass to identify an unknown landmark that you cannot reach—for example, a distant mountain peak that you would like to identify. First, determine your position with the receiver and mark it on your map. Using the

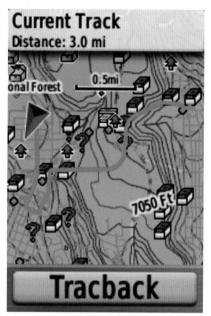

Using Garmin's "Tracback" to navigate back along your saved track

compass, take a bearing on the landmark and plot it on your map by drawing a line from your present position to the landmark. Now travel far enough so that you are looking at the unknown landmark from a different angle—the closer to 90 degrees you are from the first position, the better. Use the GPS receiver to get your new position, and mark it on the map. Take another compass sight on the landmark, and plot the bearing line on the map. The two lines will intersect at the landmark.

Chapter Eight

Hiking the Cabin Loop

A backcountry trip involves three navigational steps—planning the trip and setting up the necessary waypoints and routes at home, finding the trailhead, and navigating the trails and routes in the backcountry. In this chapter, I'll describe a scenario where you want to find Pinchot Cabin, a trailhead and historic cabin on the forested Mogollon Plateau country of central Arizona. From there you want to use three historic trails to do a nice loop hike.

Planning the Drive to Pinchot Cabin

We'll now set up a route in your GPS receiver to help you navigate to the trailhead. All routes must have a starting and ending waypoint, and you will need intermediate waypoints unless you plan to travel in a straight line. GPS receivers can store many routes, each consisting of multiple waypoints. Also, routes can be reversed for the return trip so that you do not have to reenter the route data to backtrack.

The route-editing feature on your GPS receiver allows you to create a new route and edit an existing route. You can add, change, or delete waypoints. The route-editing screen usually shows the direction and distance to each waypoint from the preceding one as well as the total distance of the route. This is valuable information for trip planning even if you do not actually use the GPS to navigate. (Keep in mind that the total distance shown on the route screen is shorter than the actual road or trail distance on the ground.) Moreover, most receivers remember an active route even when they are turned off; they resume navigating the route the next time they are turned on.

To create the driving route to Pinchot Cabin, look at a map to find your start and end points: the turnoff from Arizona Highway 87 and the historic cabin, respectively. Enter them in the receiver. Then enter a waypoint for each major road junction between the highway turnoff and your destination.

Next, create a new route using the waypoints you just entered. Refer to your GPS receiver's manual for the specific procedure. Once you have established the route, name it AZ87-PINCHOT.

If this route involved a loop with a cherrystem (a section of the route traveled both ways), the GPS receiver might get confused and be unable to tell whether you are outbound or inbound. To avoid ambiguity in such situations, break the route into two parts in the receiver. End the first route partway around the loop section, and start the second route with the last waypoint of the first route.

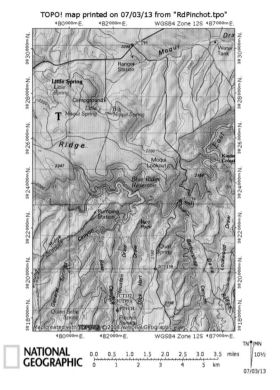

Waypoints on the road to Pinchot Cabin

Driving Route to Pinchot Cabin

Waypoint	Action
JCT95	Turn right onto Forest Road 95, a maintained dirt road
JCT96	Turn right to stay on FR 95
JCT139	Go straight ahead, remaining on FR 95
JCT132	Turn left on Forest Road 132, which may or may not be maintained
JCT95A	Turn left again on Forest Road 95A, the unmaintained spur road to the cabin
PINCH	Historic cabin

Planning the Cabin Loop Hike

You are ready to plan a hiking route on the Cabin Loop trails, which start from Pinchot Cabin. This system of recently retraced US Forest Service (USFS) trails follows the route of three historic trails that date from pioneer days.

You know from talking to an experienced friend that the trails can be hard to find. The terrain is a pine-forested plateau cut by numerous shallow canyons. The broad ridges between the canyons have been logged in the past and are laced with a network of forest roads. In some places the route follows old roads, and in other places, it follows blazes on the trees. The trail is distinct in some sections but faint or nonexistent in others. Due to the length of the loop, you plan to do it as an overnight hike, allowing plenty of time for the approach drive and time to explore the historic sites along the route. Because most of the canyons are dry, it is important that you find the springs along the route. You would also like to find the historic cabins and old trail construction that is still present at some of the canyon crossings.

Before leaving home you use the two US Geological Survey (USGS) topographic maps of the area, Dane Canyon and Blue Ridge Reservoir, to outline the trails as well as you can. (The trails are not shown on the topo maps.) With a Universal Transverse Mercator (UTM) grid reader, you create waypoints at the critical points and then name them appropriately. You also make notes to remind yourself of each waypoint's purpose once you are in the field.

As mentioned earlier, you can also create the waypoints from the map screen, if you have a mapping GPS receiver with 1:24,000 scale maps installed for the area.

The first waypoint you enter is PINCH; it marks the trailhead near Pinchot Cabin, the first historic site. During the hike you will be able to gauge your progress around the loop by checking the distance and direction to PINCH. The next waypoint, BARBER, marks the point where the U-Bar Trail crosses Barbershop Canyon. You know that the section of trail leading to Barbershop Canyon is actually just an easy-to-lose line of tree blazes in the forest. You want to make sure you find the crossing, which has a fine example of the original trail construction dating from more than a hundred years ago.

Beyond the crossing the trail intermittently follows several roads and then passes McClintock Spring. You put a waypoint, MCCLNT, at the spring. Next, the trail crosses Dane Canyon, another historic section of the old trail. There is permanent water flow here, so you mark the location with the DANECN waypoint. Now the U-Bar Trail turns south along the rim of Dane Canyon, passing Dane Spring and the ruins of another old cabin. You mark the spring with another waypoint: DANESP. About 2 miles farther south, the U-Bar Trail ends at its junction with the Barbershop Trail, near Coyote Spring. You name this junction COYOTE.

Here you want to take a short side trip to Buck Springs Cabin, less than a mile to the east, and find a nearby spring. You mark the site with a waypoint called BUCK.

The main hike continues west along the Barbershop Trail, which crosses the heads of several canyons. The most important of these is Barbershop Canyon. Though you expect the canyon to be dry at this point, Barbershop Spring is located a few hundred yards west of the main drainage. This spring is important because you may not find water again until near the trailhead. You mark the spring with the BARSPR waypoint. Less than a mile beyond the spring, you cross a dirt road and then meet the Houston Brothers Trail. Because this will be your return trail, you mark it with the HBTR waypoint.

The trail turns north along Telephone Ridge, paralleling the road, and then crosses a branch road and drops into shallow Houston Draw. To stay on the historic route, you must start down into the correct drainage, so you mark this waypoint with the name HDRAW. You place your final waypoint at Aspen Spring and call it ASPEN. When you pass the spring, you will be about a mile from the trailhead at PINCH.

Finally, you use all of the waypoints to create a route named CABIN LOOP, which reads PINCH, BARBER, MCCLNT, DANECN, DANESP, COYOTE, BUCK, COYOTE, BARSPR, HBTR, HDRAW, ASPEN, and PINCH. Note that COYOTE is entered twice because you will backtrack after BUCK. Because the hike is a loop, PINCH is the route's starting and ending waypoint.

Cabin Loop Hike Waypoints

Waypoint	Description
PINCH	Pinchot Cabin and the trailhead
BARBER	Barbershop Canyon; cross and look for historic trail construction on both sides
MCCLNT	McClintock Spring, a possible water source; exact route of trail not known in this area
DANECN	Dane Canyon; permanent water and historic trail construction here
DANESP	Old cabin and possible water source; should be an access road to this point
COYOTE	Junction with Barbershop Trail; go left for side trip to Buck Springs Cabin; on return, look for Coyote Spring a few yards west

BUCK	Buck Springs Cabin and spring
BARSPR	Barbershop Spring; pick up water here and plan to camp a short distance beyond
HBTR	Junction with Houston Brothers Trail; turn right
HDRAW	Houston Draw; trail crosses a road and descends; must find correct draw
ASPEN	Historic spring
PINCH	Pinchot Cabin and the trailhead

Driving to the Pinchot Cabin Trailhead

Now you'll use the waypoints and route that you created earlier to find Pinchot Cabin via the Forest Road system. After connecting your GPS receiver to your car's power outlet, you turn on the receiver. Assuming that you have some miles to go to reach the highway turnoff (waypoint JCT95), you use the GoTo function and the map screen to track your progress toward the junction.

You should use a highway map and a forest map to navigate to the turnoff, but the GPS display provides additional information that is useful as you drive. Knowing the bearing and distance to JCT95 allows you to gauge your progress. Your track should generally be the same as the bearing, allowing for twists and turns in the road. A large discrepancy in your track might mean

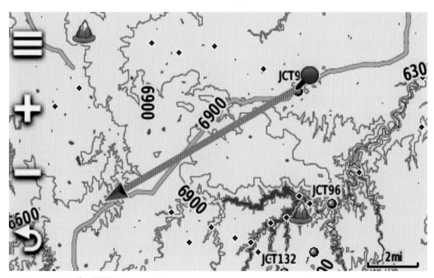

Navigating to the JCT95 waypoint

that you have taken a wrong turn. The estimated time of arrival (ETA) at the turnoff is based on your present rate of travel. The ETA changes constantly as your track and speed change, so you will need to average it over time. You can check your velocity made good (VMG) to see how fast you are actually traveling toward JCT95.

The most useful piece of information that the receiver provides is the distance to the waypoint. When you get within a mile or so, you know to start watching for the turnoff. Most receivers have an arrival alarm that sounds or flashes to signal that you are approaching the destination waypoint. An audible alarm is especially useful if you do not have a passenger to navigate for you.

After turning right onto FR 95, you activate the AZ87-PINCHOT route. The receiver detects that you are between the JCT95 and JCT96 waypoints and correctly assumes that you want to navigate from JCT95 to JCT96. Again, you gauge your progress using the map screen. The plot or map screen shows your actual track as you follow the road and the desired track from JCT95 to JCT96. You know that the next turn will be onto a maintained road, so you ignore all of the minor side roads.

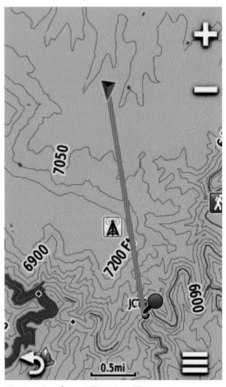

The arrival alarm warns that you are approaching JCT96, and the receiver says that you are 250 feet from it. (Most receivers change from miles to feet when you near a waypoint.) There are no road signs at the junction. Stopping to check your notes, you see that you should turn right. The map screen on the GPS receiver has jumped to the next waypoint, JCT139, and it gives a bearing of 202 degrees.

Navigating from JCT95 to JCT96

Your current track is 162 degrees, confirming that you should turn right. Some map screens will let you display turn information, which the receiver automatically computes as the difference between the bearing to the waypoint and your actual track. Your turn display says you should turn 40 degrees right. The forest map agrees, so you turn right and continue.

At the next road junction, JCT139, the receiver tells you to turn 34 degrees right. Your notes say to go straight ahead to remain on FR 95. You continue to go straight and follow FR 95 as it curves right.

When you reach the next waypoint, JCT132, you know from your notes and the GPS receiver to turn left. You do not know whether FR 132 is a major or minor road, or if it is signed. In addition, the map shows quite a few side roads in the area, and you know that you are close to the cabin. To make it easier to navigate to the cabin, you switch to the plot page and zoom the display to 0.5 mile. Now you can clearly see

Approaching the trailhead

your present position at JCT132 and the final two waypoints, including the cabin. FR 132 turns out to be an unmarked minor road; you turn left.

You know that the next turnoff, waypoint JCT95A, is an obscure, unsigned road, so you watch the receiver carefully, find the turnoff, and go left. Now the receiver shows that the cabin is just 0.2 mile ahead. The road winds down a slope into a shallow draw, and there on the edge of a meadow is the old cabin.

Hiking the Cabin Loop

At the Pinchot Cabin trailhead, switch on the receiver and allow it extra time to get a good fix. Check that the GPS accuracy is 33 feet or less to make sure your GPS location is as accurate as possible, and then save a waypoint as TRAILH.

Next you check the accuracy of the PINCH waypoint that you entered at home. (In most receivers you can do this by selecting the waypoint from the waypoint list.) Either the waypoint page or the waypoint list will show the bearing and distance to the waypoint from your current position, which lets you check its accuracy. In this case it shows that you are 30 feet from PINCH, which is close enough. As another check, you look at the TRAILH waypoint that you just saved. It shows a distance of 18 feet, still within the accuracy limits. You now have two waypoints marked at the trailhead that you can use to find your way back, if necessary.

You activate the CABIN LOOP route that you created earlier. Switching to the map screen, you change the scale so that you can see the entire route. This serves as double confirmation that you did not enter any waypoints incorrectly. If a waypoint was off by a large amount, it would be obvious on the map screen. You zoom the map to the 5-mile scale, which shows the next waypoint, BARBER. In doing so you notice that the screen is cluttered by the track you made on the drive to the trailhead, so you use the "clear track" function from the receiver's menu to erase the old track. Now the only lines on the map screen are the desired track lines between waypoints on the Cabin Loop.

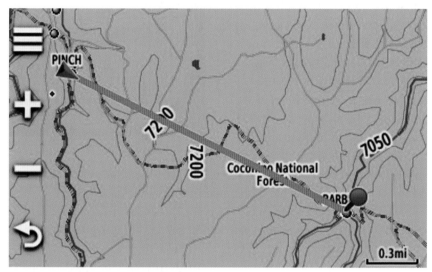

Starting navigation on the CABIN LOOP route

With the GPS receiver turned off but handy in its case on your belt, you start up the U-Bar Trail. The trail climbs up the east side of the draw onto the forested plateau. The tread is distinct, and you note the blazes on the trees. Before long the trail merges with an old road; you follow the road, keeping an eye out for blazes. Another road soon joins from the left, and a few yards farther on, the tree blazes suddenly veer left, away from the road. There is no sign of trail tread on the flat, needle-carpeted forest floor. You turn on the GPS and check the direction to BARBER. Judging by the position of the sun, the blazes look as if they are headed in the right direction, but you get out your compass and check the bearing to BARBER to confirm. As a precaution, you save your current position as a waypoint, letting the receiver automatically name it 001. You note the waypoint on your topographic map. This waypoint will allow you to find this junction again—the last place where you knew you were definitely on the trail.

Turning the receiver off, you follow the blazes east through the pine forest. The route crosses a major drainage, and about half an hour later, a major dirt road shown on the map. You follow the blazes for a short distance, then lose them in an area of freshly downed trees. You check the receiver for the bearing and distance to BARBER. You are less than half a mile from the canyon crossing. Anxious to find the trail again so that you do not miss the trail construction in Barbershop Canyon, you use your compass to walk the bearing to BARBER. Soon you reach the rim of the small canyon. There is no sign of the trail. Checking the receiver again, you see that BARBER is upstream, or south, of your location. You decide to walk the rim to see if you can intercept the trail. Sure enough, you find the blazed route again and obvious trail construction. You mark this spot as waypoint 002, making a note on your map to remind you of its purpose.

The trail is clear as it descends into the canyon and you take some photos of the old trail construction. At the bottom you take a rest break by the stream and check your position with the receiver. The BARBER waypoint is only 150 feet from your location, so you do not need to save a new waypoint. After a while you follow the trail as it climbs out the east side of the canyon. The blazes are easy to follow even after the trail construction disappears on the

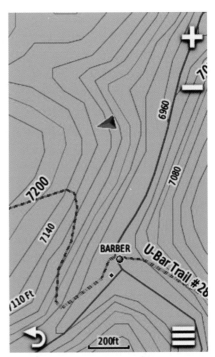

Checking the location of BARBER

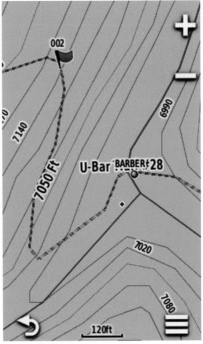

Waypoint 002 along CABIN LOOP

pine flats. It is less than a mile to McClintock Spring, so you keep an eye on the time. After half an hour, you will have traveled a mile and should be near the spring, so you stop and check the receiver. It is now navigating to MCCLNT, the next waypoint on the route. It shows the spring bearing east at 89 degrees true and 0.3 mile away. The trail, however, is heading southeast at 140 degrees. Leaving the receiver on, you walk along the trail until the spring bears 45 degrees and is 0.25 mile away. It becomes clear that the spring is a short distance from the trail but not actually on it.

Deciding to find the spring and refill your water bottles, you save a waypoint to mark your location

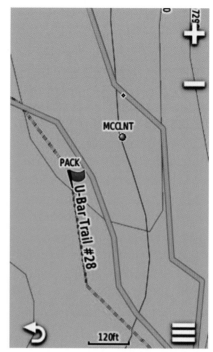

MCCLNT as shown just off the trail

and name it PACK. You leave your pack beside a blazed tree but take the GPS receiver, map, and compass. You walk northeast through the forest and find the spring in less than fifteen minutes. After filling your bottles, you activate GoTo navigation to PACK and note the bearing, 227 degrees, and the distance, 0.28 mile. Using the sun to estimate the direction, you walk southwest to return to your pack.

You continue along the trail, following it across Dane Canyon and then south along the rim. The trail is distinct in this section, but you are concerned that you might miss the old cabin at Dane Spring if it is not on the trail, as was the case with McClintock Spring. You check the receiver after about forty-five minutes of walking, and it shows DANESP 0.45 mile distant at a bearing of 168 degrees. Your compass shows that the trail is heading almost directly toward the spring, at 166 degrees, so you expect to find it very near the trail (unless the trail turns). Sure enough, after another twenty minutes of walking, you find the spring and the ruins of the cabin at the end of a spur road.

Continuing along the U-Bar Trail as it heads south, you occasionally use the receiver to check your progress toward the next waypoint, COYOTE. You would like to reach the spring near the junction with the Barbershop Trail in time for lunch. You reach the trail junction and find the spring a couple hundred yards to the west. After lunch you leave your pack and follow the trail east to Buck Springs Cabin, which you find without difficulty. After exploring the cabin and nearby spring, you check your position with the receiver and find that the BUCK waypoint is correct. You hike back to your pack and continue east on the Barbershop Trail.

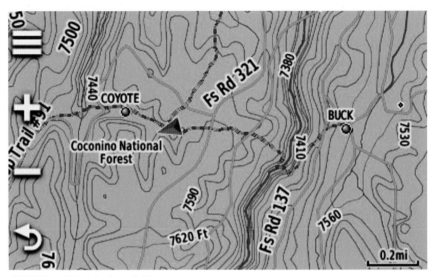

COYOTE and Buck Springs Cabin

The trail, now mostly just a line of blazed trees, wanders through an area of shallow draws laced with numerous old roads. Finally, you lose the trail entirely. Stopping at the last blazed tree you are able to find, you turn on the receiver and save your position as waypoint 003. After looking at the topographic map, you decide to hike cross-country directly to Barbershop Spring, your planned campsite. The terrain is nearly flat, and you will have only a few shallow canyons to cross. The receiver shows that the BARSPR waypoint is at 230 degrees, 1.2 miles away. You use your compass to check the direction, then set out.

Cross-country travel is easy through the open forest. You have been walking for just over half an hour

Hiking from 003 to BARSPR

when, descending into one of the shallow canyons, you spot the ruins of a log cabin alongside the drainage. The old structure is not marked on the topographic map. Checking the area, you cannot find a road or trail leading to the cabin site. You would like to spend some time exploring, but it is late afternoon and time presses, so you save your position on the receiver as a waypoint named RUIN. You also mark the location on your topographic map using the UTM coordinates shown on the display. You plan to return later and use the saved waypoint to find the old cabin.

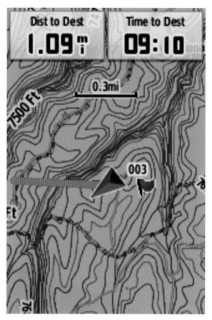

Marking RUIN

Resuming your cross-country walk toward Barbershop Spring, you walk for about twenty minutes before checking your progress on the receiver. The spring is now 0.3 mile away, and the map shows that you should be crossing a major dirt road very shortly. At the road there is still no sign of the trail. On the far side of the road you descend into a shallow canyon; this is probably the head of Barbershop Canyon. The GPS display confirms this hypothesis. As you continue toward the spring, you leave the receiver on. When it shows you already at the spring, you are standing on dry forest floor, but a shallow ravine lies ahead. As you descend into the ravine, you find a faint trail and distinct blazes on the trees leading

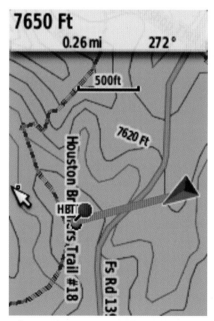

Hiking to the Houston Brothers Trail junction at HBTR

to the west. You find the spring in the ravine and fill your water bottles. It is a damp, buggy place, and you prefer not to camp near springs anyway, so you

Cabin Loop Hike

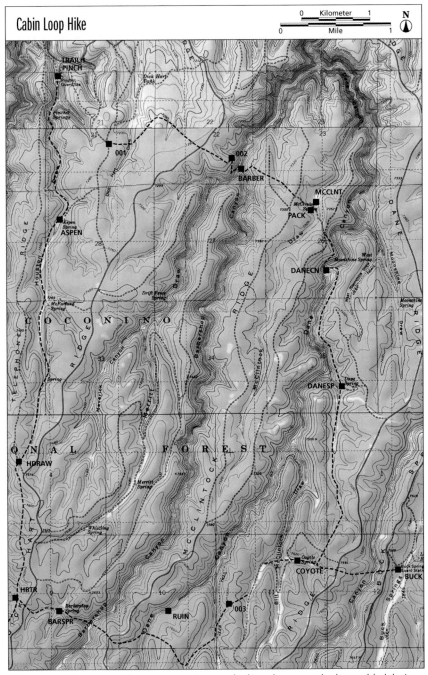

Cabin Loop hike route, with some waypoints marked in advance and others added during hike

hike a few hundred yards west on the trail and find a place to camp out of sight of both the trail and the spring.

The next morning, back on the trail, you check the receiver. The distance and bearing to the junction with the Houston Brothers Trail (waypoint HBTR) should be 0.5 mile west, and the receiver confirms that. The trail crosses a road, and you find the junction on the other side. You turn right and hike north. The next waypoint, HDRAW, marks the point where the trail descends into Houston Draw. The trail remains distinct, and you locate the head of the draw without difficulty. Nevertheless, you are glad that you saved the waypoint as a backup.

You know that Pinchot Cabin, the trailhead, is located in Houston Draw, so all you have to do is follow the draw north to reach it. Still, there are few landmarks in the upper part of the draw, so you check your progress on the receiver from time to time. You also want to make sure that you find Aspen Spring. After an hour of steady hiking, you find a spring in an aspen grove. There is no sign, so you use the receiver to confirm that you are really at Aspen Spring. From here it is an easy walk of less than a mile to Pinchot Cabin and the trailhead.

Chapter Nine

Exploring a Desert Mountain Range

GPS is especially handy when you are hiking or exploring cross-country. In the next example, a cross-country hike in the desert, you want to explore a desert mountain range that looks interesting. According to your topographic map, the nearest access is a dirt road that loosely parallels the northwest-southeast trending range about 5 miles to the east. The only water source you know of is a natural stone tank that holds rainwater. It has been a wet winter so far, so the tank should be full, and now in late winter the desert weather is dry and cool—perfect for hiking. You plan to take three days on the trip because of the long walk across the desert plain to reach the foot of the range.

Entering Waypoints in Advance

Because you do not know where you will want to park along the approach road, you cannot place a waypoint in advance. However, you do have a map location for the natural water tank, obtained from a ranger. Finding the water is critical to the success of your trip, so you carefully determine the Universal Transverse Mercator (UTM) coordinates from your topo map and enter a waypoint called TANK into your GPS receiver. The tank is near the southern end of the section of the range you would like to explore, so you plan to hike to the tank and then explore generally to the north before returning to your vehicle. Because of the length of the approach drive, you probably will not make it to the tank the first night, so you plan to carry enough water for a dry camp.

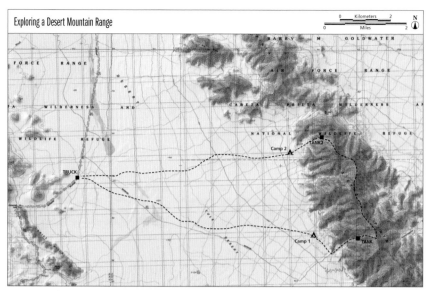

Waypoints for exploring a desert mountain range

Finding Your Starting Point

As you drive along the desert road, you turn on the receiver and set up TANK as a GoTo route. Then you switch to the map screen and zoom until you can see both your present position and TANK. This allows you to see where you are in relation to the tank. You park your truck where the road makes its closest approach to TANK. Given that your GPS receiver has been running

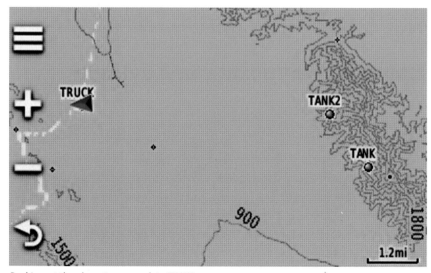

Parking at the closest approach to TANK

continuously on the vehicle's power, you know that it should have a good position fix. After making sure that the receiver is locked on to at least four satellites and that there are no warning messages, you save your position as a waypoint named TRUCK. You also plot your position on your map and write the coordinates on the map margin.

Hiking to Your First Waypoint

Next you check the GPS map screen, which is still telling you the bearing and distance to the tank. You use your compass to sight along the GPS bearing to the tank, and you note a peak along the crest of the distant range. You will use the peak for general guidance as you cross the desert plain. You stash the GPS receiver and compass in your pack and start hiking. The otherwise flat plain is cut by numerous dry washes, so you constantly make small detours, but focusing on the distant peak keeps you heading in the right direction. As expected, the setting sun forces you to stop and camp just before you reach the foothills. Checking the GPS receiver, you see that the tank is about a mile away.

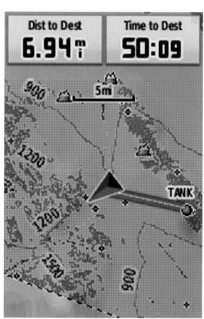

Bearing and distance to TANK from your truck

Avoiding Rough Terrain

In the morning you check the GPS bearing to TANK and use your compass to find the direction. The terrain between you and the tank looks rugged, so you skirt it to the south. When you've hiked 30 minutes and should be about halfway to the tank, you switch on the receiver, check the bearing and distance, and then hike directly toward the tank. You find it easily, located in the mouth of an open canyon at the foot of the range, and it is a welcome sight in the otherwise dry mountains. You check that the TANK waypoint is accurately located and then continue north along the range. Since your plan is to hike up to the crest of the range above the tank and climb the highest peak, you navigate by the terrain and do not use your GPS.

Marking a New Water Source

After climbing the peak, you head north along the crest of the range. Since you're generally following the ridge top, working with the terrain and the topo to find the easy route, your GPS receiver stays in your pack. After several miles, you come to a section where the crest becomes much more broken and difficult. Since the sun is getting lower in the west, you decide to descend a ridge to the northwest. Near the foothills, it becomes easier to drop into the dry wash just south of the ridge. As you walk down the dry wash, it enters a short narrows and you encounter an unexpected surprise, a stone tank holding hundreds of gallons of water, hidden within the short, narrow canyon. Grateful for the excuse to take a break, you drop

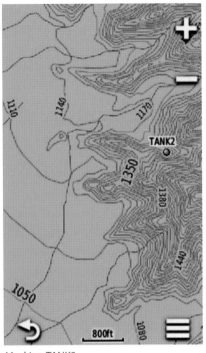

Marking TANK2

your pack and fill your water bottles. Even though you had enough water for a dry camp, it's always good to fill up. After a drink and a snack, you pull out the GPS and switch it on.

After several minutes, the receiver still hasn't locked on to the satellites. Apparently the receiver's view of the sky is too restricted in the narrow canyon, so you walk down the canyon about 0.25 mile to where it opens out. The GPS receiver gets a solid lock so you save a waypoint as TANK2, and make a note on your map that the actual tank lies 0.25 mile upstream of the waypoint.

The setting sun hastens you on your way, so you retrieve your pack and walk on down the wash until it opens out into the desert plain. Soon you find a nice campsite and settle in for your well-deserved dinner. As you eat, you catch up on your notes, marking your route of travel up to this point on your topo map and describing the terrain you hiked.

Returning to Your Vehicle

In the morning you use the GPS receiver to determine the direction and distance to your truck across the gently sloping desert plain. Since there are no landmarks in that direction, you maintain your course using the position of the sun. You are not concerned about maintaining exact direction because you know that the terrain will force you off course anyway. Sure enough, the flat-appearing plain is cut up by shallow dry washes, each of which requires a detour to find a way down, across, and back up again. You walk almost directly west and then slightly northwest before the going becomes easier. Taking a break, you again use the receiver to find the direction to your truck. This time you keep the receiver and compass handy as you hike because the desert is nearly flat, and you can see only about half a mile ahead because of the low ridges and shallow washes. You maintain your course with the compass, stopping to check your progress occasionally with the receiver. Soon you spot your truck.

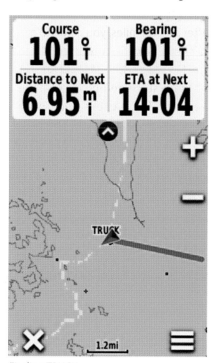

Finding TRUCK

Although this hike certainly could have been done without GPS, satellite navigation made it easier and faster to find the critical water tank. It also freed you to explore at will along the range, knowing that you could descend out of the mountains and hike directly to your vehicle at any time. Without GPS you would have had to keep track of your position carefully and deliberately hike toward a point well to one side of your truck so that you would know which way to turn when you hit the road. Finally, with GPS, you were able to mark the exact location of the second water tank; having this information will make it easier to explore the northern section of the range on a later trip.

Chapter Ten

Mapping a Mountain Bike Trail

In this example you will use a GPS receiver with a data cable and a personal computer with ExpertGPS to plan a new mountain bike trail. (ExpertGPS works with standard GPX files and free topo maps, street maps, and aerial imagery downloaded from the Internet.) The object is to help your local mountain bike club plan and map a new bike trail in cooperation with the US Forest Service. The proposed trail wanders through dense forest with few landmarks. The Forest Service wants a map of the proposed route before it is constructed and a final, detailed map of the trail after it is finished. The club also wants a good map of the trail for its members and other riders.

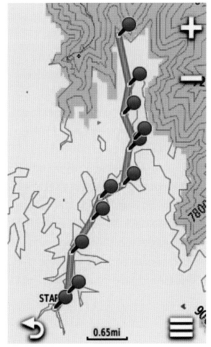

Planned mountain bike trail

Planning the Trail

Your plan is to start the trail from a gravel road and run it through the forest to a viewpoint. On your personal computer, you use ExpertGPS to display a map of the proposed route. Then you create a new GPS route using the route tool. Left-click the mouse on the proposed start of the trail along the dirt road. From here, you want to run the trail across a series of drainages to create a "roller coaster" section that is fun but not too technical. Continue to click on the map to create new waypoints and add them to the route. ExpertGPS automatically names the waypoints as you add them. Mark the last waypoint at the viewpoint, then right-click to end the route.

Now rename the start and end waypoints START and VIEWPOINT. Rename the intermediate waypoints MB001, MB002, through MB010. Finally, using the route editor, name the route VIEWTRAIL. You save the waypoints and route on your computer as ViewPointTrail.gpx.

Downloading Data

You connect the GPS receiver to your computer and download the route and waypoints to the GPS. Next, you print the map for use in the field.

In the Field

You use the GoTo function on your receiver to navigate directly to START. That way, as you drive the approach road through the dense forest, you will know when you have reached the proposed start of the trail. When you arrive at START, you see right away that it is not a good trailhead because there is no place to park. You passed a section of road with a wide shoulder about half a mile back, so you turn around. As you expected, there is room for

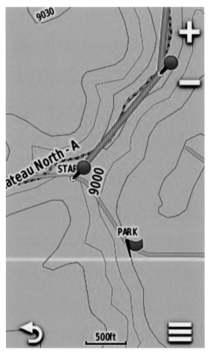

The planned START waypoint and the actual starting point, PARK

several cars to park, so you stop the car, grab your pack, turn on your GPS receiver, and save your location as a waypoint named PARK.

Mapping the Proposed Trail

You need a section of trail to connect PARK to the rest of the planned trail, so after looking at the map you decide to check out the area to the west of PARK. A few hundred yards of thrashing your way through deadfall and brush convinces you that the club members who will build the trail will not be happy if you route the trail there. You check out area east of PARK. It is much better—the forest is fairly open, and the terrain is just right for an easy roller-coaster trail. You save a waypoint, letting the receiver name it 001.

Now you need to connect waypoint 001 to the rest of the planned trail. You use the GoTo function to navigate directly to MB002, the closest waypoint on the planned trail. When you reach MB002, you activate the VIEWTRAIL route. This starts navigation to MB002. As you go, you mark more key points where you want the trail to run. By the time you reach VIEWPOINT, you have created waypoints 001 through 007 to mark the exact route of the planned trail.

Uploading the Field Waypoints

Back at home, you upload all of the waypoints from the GPS receiver to your computer, then use the track tool in ExpertGPS to draw in the trail along the waypoints. This gives you a provisional map to print for the Forest Service. Delete the unused START waypoint, print the map, and save the file.

Creating the Final Route

After the Forest Service approves the route, you use the ExpertGPS route tool to create a new route on your computer with all of your field waypoints; you call this route APPROVEDTRAIL to distinguish it from your original planned trail. Then you copy and paste all of the waypoints into the route to create the final map for trail construction. After deleting the old VIEWTRAIL route, you activate the APPROVEDTRAIL route, save the file, download the route and waypoints to your GPS receiver, and print the map.

In the field it is easy to navigate along the APPROVEDTRAIL route. You mark the trail with flags for the club members to follow while the trail is under construction.

Mapping the Constructed Trail

After the trail is complete, you ride it with your GPS receiver turned on and set to save a track log. You also save as many waypoints as you need to map each twist and turn. And you use a cyclometer to measure distances between key points on the trail. The cyclometer will measure trail distance more accurately because it follows each twist and turn on the trail. After uploading the waypoints to your computer, you create a final map for both club riders and the Forest Service. Of course, the Forest Service is so impressed with your trail-planning ability that it immediately asks for your club's assistance with another trail project!

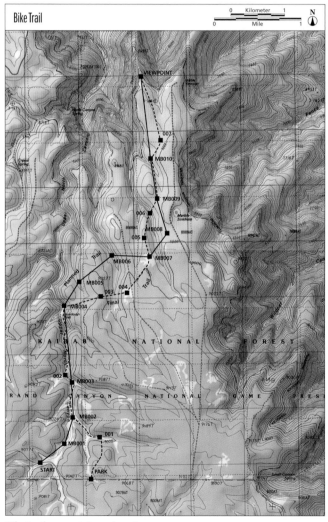

Bike trail waypoints and route

Chapter 11

Relocating Your Favorite Fishing Spot

For flatwater navigation, it helps to mount your receiver so that you can check it easily. You do not need to leave it on all the time; you can just turn it on for position and course checks. Although most GPS receivers are waterproof to varying degrees, don't trust that to protect the unit. Also, most GPS receivers don't float if accidentally dropped overboard. Get a waterproof bag with a transparent window that is made specifically for hand-held GPS receivers. Most bags will mount on the deck of a sea kayak or can be secured to the thwarts of a canoe. Note that touchscreen GPS receivers can't be operated inside a waterproof bag.

Planning the Route

Let's say that you want to paddle your canoe across a large lake to reach a favorite fishing spot and campsite on the far side. The distance is about 5 miles, and there are no landmarks on the far shore to steer by. Last time you were there, you saved a waypoint called FISH at the spot. Before setting out, save your launching point as a waypoint called LAUNCH; then create and activate a route from LAUNCH to FISH. As you paddle, the map screen shows the bearing and distance to your goal. You can use the track information to stay on course, turning until your track and the bearing agree, but an easier method is to use the course deviation indicator (CDI) setting on the compass screen of your GPS.

Normally, the compass screen on the GPS has a pointer that always points directly toward the next waypoint. A CDI, on the other hand, has an offset bar within the bearing pointer that represents your course, relative to your current position. This CDI is usually a horizontal row of dots with a vertical bar and arrow. The bar moves left or right to show how far off course you are. You can change the scale of the CDI in the setup page. The CDI is not useful for land travel but is helpful for direct point-to-point travel on the water. If current or wind moves you off course, you can see immediately which way to turn to get back on course.

Using the Course Deviation Indicator

Set the CDI to its most sensitive scale. When you are on course, the course bar is centered within the bearing arrow. If you get off course, the course bar moves to the side. To correct any deviation, make a small change in your heading toward the course bar and see if the CDI starts to center. If not, make another small heading change. When the CDI starts to move toward center, hold that heading until it has centered. Don't make large changes or you will find yourself zigzagging through your course.

Cross Track Error

The cross track error (XTK) display shows distance off course. On most GPS receivers, you can customize the map or compass screen to show XTK. You can use XTK to help you decide how far to turn to get back on course. For example, if your destination is 5 miles away and your XTK is 0.1 mile, make a 10-degree turn to get back on course. If your XTK is 1 mile and you have 5 miles to go, turn 30 degrees to get back on course. The idea is to get back on course without going too far out of your way.

Effects of Wind and Current

If you have wind or current from one side, you will be carried off course even though your heading is the same as the bearing to the waypoint. In this case, steer a few degrees into the wind or current to compensate. Check the CDI occasionally; if you are off course, adjust your heading toward your desired course. If the wind or current is steady, you will be able to find a heading that will keep you exactly on course, so that you paddle the shortest distance to your destination.

Estimated Time of Arrival

It can be difficult to judge distance on water, but the estimated time of arrival (ETA) display can help measure your progress. Remember that ETA is based on your speed made good and the distance remaining to your waypoint. If you frequently wander off course or slow down, your ETA will change.

Keep in mind that the heading and ETA displays may be inaccurate at low speeds on older GPS receivers; do not make constant course changes in response to small changes in the display. If a distant landmark is available, steer by it to stay on course; otherwise, use a compass.

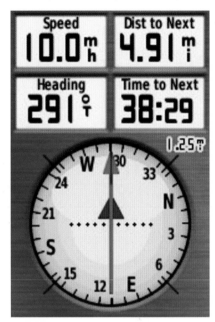

Estimated time of arrival (ETA)

Chapter 12

Advanced GPS

GPS offers additional features that are likely to be of interest to backcountry users: geocaching, the Automatic Position Reporting System (APRS), Differential GPS (DGPS), and the Wide Area Augmentation System (WAAS). In addition, the US military is testing battlefield spoofing and jamming systems designed to disrupt an enemy's ability to use GPS. Other applications for GPS, such as surveying and land management, are beyond the scope of this book. Refer to the appendix for books on these subjects.

Geocaching

Geocaching as a sport actually predates the GPS system, but GPS is a natural match. The idea is to find geocaches that others have placed, and then record your find in the logbook in the geocache, and also online. Geocaching.com is the most popular website for geocachers; opencaching.com is an open, free site that is gaining in popularity.

Automatic Position Reporting System

APRS is an amateur radio system that uses digital radio to track objects. APRS stations can be fixed, mobile, or portable, so the system can track all types of vehicles and even people. Since the system uses radio communications, it can transmit general messages as well as specialized information. The Internet also can be used to link APRS stations, so an amateur radio license is not required for those who use the system. An APRS station uses a computer to display a map with the positions of all other APRS stations. Weather data and message traffic also can be displayed.

Amateur radio operators are using APRS to provide communications and position tracking in disaster situations and for public service events such as races and parades. The Civil Air Patrol uses APRS to help it search for overdue aircraft. For more information, visit aprs.net.

Differential GPS

Each GPS satellite transmits three primary navigation signals: the coarse/acquisition code (C/A), the precise code (P), and the navigation signal. Your receiver uses this information to compute its position. Errors creep into the calculated position because of small errors in the satellite positions, variations in radio wave propagation through the atmosphere, and other factors. DGPS overcomes most of these inaccuracies by using a GPS receiver and a DGPS beacon transmitter placed on a known, surveyed point. The transmitter continuously computes the difference between its known position and its GPS position, and transmits the correction. Field GPS receivers equipped with a DGPS receiver pick up this signal and correct their location accordingly. DGPS positioning can be accurate to a few millimeters.

DGPS is more complex and costly than the basic system because a DGPS beacon receiver must be attached to the normal GPS receiver. The system works only within range of a DGPS beacon transmitter.

DGPS is routinely used in surveying and will become increasingly important in navigation. The US Coast Guard maintains a network of DGPS stations to improve the accuracy of marine navigation near the coast. The US Forest Service, the US Bureau of Land Management, other federal agencies, and private citizens use DGPS locally to improve the accuracy of their survey and mapping operations.

Wide Area Augmentation System

The Federal Aviation Administration (FAA) built WAAS, a differential GPS system, to improve the accuracy of GPS for aircraft between destinations. The FAA uses a similar system, the Local Area Augmentation System (LAAS), for precision instrument approaches—to help aircraft find a runway in bad weather, for example. Tests have demonstrated an LAAS accuracy of better than two centimeters. Another function of both WAAS and LAAS is to warn flight crews of degraded accuracy or GPS failure. Such warnings are critical when GPS is used to guide a fast-moving aircraft to within a few feet of a runway.

WAAS consists of a series of geostationary satellites located over the equator and ground reference stations that cover North America. The system transmits on current GPS frequencies, so it is available to anyone with a receiver capable of using WAAS information. Such receivers have an accuracy of 3 to 5 meters (10 to 16 feet) horizontally and 3 to 7 meters (10 to 23 feet) vertically. Although backcountry users do not really need this degree of accuracy, most hand-held receivers are now WAAS-enabled. Check at your receiver's satellite status page to determine whether it is accessing WAAS information.

GLONASS

GLONASS is the Russian equivalent to the US GPS system, and it is now fully operational. Although GLONASS is not compatible with GPS, some newer trail GPS units can also receive GLONASS signals. While using GLONASS with GPS doesn't appear to increase accuracy, it does help the receiver maintain a satellite lock when the sky is partially obscured.

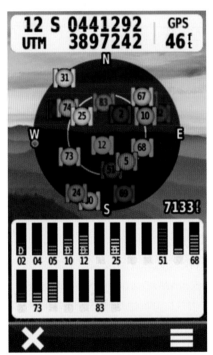

GPS receiving WAAS signals as shown by the "D" on the signal strength bar

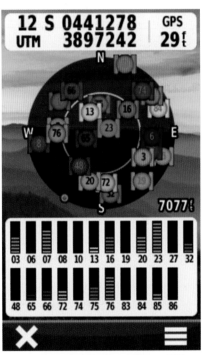

GPS receiving GLONASS satellites—GPS satellites are the top row of bars, and GLONASS the bottom

Galileo

Galileo is the European Union's satellite navigation system. Although it is fully compatible with GPS, satellites are still being launched and the Galileo system is not expected to be operational until 2019.

Military Applications

Since the US government makes GPS freely available for all users worldwide, the US military needs a way to deny the use of GPS to enemies on the battlefield. The US Department of Defense has developed a battlefield jamming system and occasionally tests it on military proving grounds. If you're using GPS near such a test site, your GPS may not work.

Chapter Thirteen

The Future of GPS

GPS grew out of the military's need for an accurate, twenty-four-hour, global, all-weather navigation system that could provide rapidly updated positions for ships, aircraft, tanks, troops, and weapons. When planning for the system started in 1973, there were several major goals. The system had to be resistant to jamming, and it had to be encrypted (i.e., the radio signals had to be encoded) so that unauthorized persons could not interfere with it. The system also needed to be passive so that users would not have to reveal their positions by transmitting. In addition, the US Congress wanted the Department of Defense to consolidate all of the existing military navigation systems into one. Civilian uses were not part of the original design, but many of the design features that make the system so useful to the military also make it attractive to civilians. The passive design means that GPS receivers are relatively simple devices, and their cost has dropped rapidly as electronic and computer technology improves.

The first GPS satellite, NAVSTAR 1, was launched in 1978; its ten sisters followed over the next few years. These early satellites were prototypes, designed to test and refine the system. Though their design life was four-and-a-half years, some lasted more than twice that long. The next generation of GPS satellites was launched in 1989. These satellites are hardened against attack by antisatellite weapons and are designed to last seven-and-a-half years. A third generation of GPS satellites have more accurate atomic clocks and use intersatellite communications to reduce dependency on updates from ground stations.

In the future, GPS technology will become commonplace. Some people are concerned that GPS and other technologies, such as cell and satellite telephones, degrade or even destroy the wilderness experience. It is not a new argument. The same concern arose when the lightweight, high-tech aluminum pack frame was invented, and ham radio has generated similar complaints. I am a lifetime amateur radio operator, and I have carried a small ham radio receiver in my pack for many years. Some of my hiking companions have objected to the intrusion of two-way radio communications into our trips. The answer, as always, is to use technology appropriately during your backcountry trip. When I hike with non-ham companions, I leave the radio out of sight in my pack, for use only in an emergency. Likewise, you can keep a GPS receiver in reserve in case your party becomes disoriented—much the way some people always carry a compass but rarely use it in open country.

Be careful not to become dependent on gadgets to get you out of trouble in wild country. In some areas—Utah's canyon country, for example, where the terrain is cut by thousands of canyons—GPS and compass navigation are not that useful. Although a GPS receiver will tell you the direction and distance to your destination in a straight line, to get there you may have to hike many more miles and work closely with the terrain and a map to avoid canyons and other obstacles. Lastly, remember that electronic devices fail. Plan to rely on your own survival knowledge in the backcountry and use your high-tech equipment only as a backup.

Appendix

GPS and Accessory Manufacturers

DeLorme
GPS receivers, SPOT receivers, maps
delorme.com

Garmin International Inc.
GPS receivers and maps
garmin.com

Lowrance Electronics
GPS receivers
lowrance.com

Magellan Systems Inc.
GPS receivers and maps
magellangps.com

RAM

GPS mounts
ram-mount.com

Trimble Navigation Limited
trimble.com

Compasses

Brunton Co.
bruntonoutdoor.com

Silva USA
silvacompass.com

Suunto USA Inc.
suunto.com

Maps and Tools

ExpertGPS.com

Computer GPS and mapping software using free, open-source maps and aerial imagery

TopoFusion.com

Computer GPS and mapping software using free, open-source maps and aerial imagery

GPSfiledepot.com

Free, open-source maps for GPS

GPStracklog.com

Trail and street GPS reviews

MapTools

Plotters and tool for use with paper maps
maptools.com

US Geological Survey, Information Services

mapping.usgs.gov

Glossary

AAA Tourbook: Street GPS units with this feature contain POI data from the Tourbooks published by the American Automobile Association.

Accuracy: Civilian GPS receivers are accurate to 10 meters (33 feet) and often achieve accuracy of 3 meters (10 feet). Accuracy varies depending on satellite geometry, number of satellites visible, atmospheric conditions, radio signal propagation, and other factors. Some GPS receivers display an accuracy figure in feet or meters. This is an estimated accuracy calculated by the internal software and varies between manufacturers. It should not be relied on or use to compare the accuracy of different receivers. But generally, a lower accuracy figure indicates more satellites in view and good satellite geometry.

Altimeter: GPS measurement of altitude is accurate to about 15 meters (49 feet) under ideal conditions. Units that have a barometric altimeter can improve on this accuracy, but the altimeter must be set to a known elevation or barometer setting.

Anti-Theft Features: On a street GPS, this feature typically allows you to set a password that must be entered in order to use the receiver. You may also be able to set a security location, which disables the unit if it is turned on at a different location.

Audio Book Player: This features enables you to play audio books through the GPS unit.

Auto Reroute: This feature, found on nearly all street GPS receivers, automatically recalculates the route if you take a wrong turn or deviate from the GPS-planned route.

Auto Orientation: On street GPS receivers, it automatically changes the screen display from landscape to portrait when you rotate the unit. Useful when you want to look ahead further along the route.

Auto Sort Multiple Destinations: This feature lets you plan the most efficient route to multiple destinations, which is useful for making deliveries or sales calls.

B/W LCD: Reflective black and white LCD screens that are now found only on wrist-top GPS receivers without mapping capability.

Basemap: All mapping trail GPS receivers and all street GPS receivers have basemaps. These maps are built into the unit and generally cover a larger area in less detail than the preloaded or loadable maps.

Batteries: Most trail receivers use common AA- or AAA-size alkaline batteries. The unit should also be able to use NiMH rechargeable and lithium single-use batteries. Lithium batteries have the longest life under outdoor conditions, but NiMH batteries can be recharged hundreds of times. Get the newer NiMH batteries that retain their charge during storage. Street GPS receivers have internal rechargeable batteries.

Battery Life: Specified in hours with the unit running continuously. Long battery life is necessary in a trail GPS. Battery life can be extended to days by leaving the unit off except when checking your position and saving waypoints. Street GPS receivers are normally run from vehicle power and the battery is used only for pre-trip planning away from the vehicle.

Bluetooth(R): This feature lets you use your Bluetooth cell phone to make hands-free calls using the microphone and speaker on the street GPS receiver.

Color TFT: Backlit transreflective color LCD screen. These screens work well in bright sunlight and are backlit for use in poor light. 256-color screens are fine for maps, but if you want to look at photos on your GPS unit, you'll want 65K color.

Compass: While all trail GPS receivers have a compass page, the GPS cannot show your direction of travel while you are stopped unless it includes a magnetic compass. A 3-axis compass works when tilted.

COMPASS: A regional satellite positioning system operated by China that currently covers Asia and the Pacific and is planned to cover the entire Earth by 2020. It is not compatible with GPS.

Coordinates: Numbers and letters describing a physical location. Most trail GPS units can use many different coordinate systems. The most common are latitude and longitude and Universal Transverse Mercator. Most street GPS units display coordinates in latitude and longitude, although it's rare that you would use coordinates instead of POIs or street addresses.

Custom Maps: Lets you add non-proprietary maps. There are now many free sources of maps, and you can scan any paper map and load it as a custom map. For mapping GPS receivers, this is an essential feature.

Custom POI: Nearly every street GPS unit (and trail GPS receivers with street maps loaded) lets you save locations and POIs as favorites. This saves time next time you need to navigate to the same location.

Dashboards: Customizable screens with presets for specific activities.

Data Cards: Many GPS receivers use flash memory cards to increase the amount of memory in the unit. If you plan to add maps or store a lot of data in your receiver, make certain it uses SDHC or MicroSD cards.

Datum: The physical reference system used to make maps, based on surveyed points on the ground. GPS is based on the World Geodetic System of 1984 (WGS84), while most US Geological Survey topographic maps are based on the North American Datum of 1927 (NAD27). Trail GPS receivers must be set to the correct datum when working with paper maps. If the wrong datum is used, GPS positions can be off by many feet or even miles.

DGPS: Differential GPS uses GPS receivers placed on accurately surveyed points to generate corrective signals and transmit them to DGPS-equipped GPS receivers. Commonly used for surveying, scientific, engineering, and navigation applications, DGPS can achieve accuracies of several millimeters.

Display Resolution: Expressed in pixels. More pixels means a higher resolution screen, allowing you to see finer map and photo details.

Emergency Location: This street GPS feature lets you quickly find the nearest emergency services, including police, fire, and medical.

Exit Services: Also called "Exit POIs," this feature shows you points of interest, including services, for upcoming freeway exits.

External Antenna Connector: If you plan to use your trail GPS extensively inside a vehicle, you may want to mount an external antenna on the roof of the vehicle for more reliable satellite reception.

Floats: Boaters may want a unit that floats, although for protection from the water, paddlers should enclose the GPS receiver in a waterproof bag. This also adds flotation to any unit.

FM Transmitter: Transmits audio from the GPS unit to your vehicle's FM radio receiver. This is especially useful for motorcyclists as they can hear the GPS prompts in their headphone-equipped helmets.

4 Level Gray: Reflective gray scale LCD screen. Color TFT screens work better in a variety of lighting conditions.

Fuel-Efficient Routing: When enabled, this street GPS feature chooses the route that will give you the best fuel economy.

Galileo: Under development by the European Union, the Galileo Positioning System will be fully compatible with GPS, increasing accuracy and reliability of existing GPS receivers. Galileo is expected to be fully operational in 2019.

GLONASS: The Global Navigation Satellite System, operated by the Russian Federation. GLONASS became fully operational in 2011. It is comparable in coverage and accuracy to GPS but requires a different receiver. Some of the newest trail GPS units have dual receiver systems and can use both GPS and GLONASS. Use of both systems increases signal reliability and accuracy.

GPX: GPX is becoming the standard file format for transferring GPS data between receivers and computers.

High-Sensitivity Receiver: Nearly all street and trail GPS receivers now have multi-channel, high-sensitivity receivers. Each channel receives one satellite, so multi-channel receivers use more satellites simultaneously. Higher sensitivity means that the GPS unit can use satellite signals that are partially blocked by foliage. This means that your receiver will work better under difficult conditions—in forest, canyons, or among high-rise buildings.

Hunt/Fish Calendar: Hunters and anglers may find this trail GPS feature useful. It attempts to predict the best times for hunting and fishing.

Interface: USB is standard. The newer USB 2.0 standard is much faster than USB 1.1 and is useful if you plan to upload many maps to your receiver.

Internal Memory: The amount of internal memory determines how many maps, POIs, waypoints, routes, tracks, and geocaches you can store in the unit. This memory cannot be increased.

Junction View: On street GPS receivers, shows a picture of the exit signs at freeway off ramps.

Landmark Guidance: Calls out landmarks such as gas stations to help you find turns. Can be misleading because landmarks change far more frequently than street names. Don't buy a street GPS receiver with this feature unless it can be disabled.

Lane Guidance: This feature assists you in choosing the correct lane for an upcoming exit or turn.

Lifetime Map Updates: Free map updates for the life of the receiver. Otherwise, you'll have to buy and manually upload map updates. But also consider that map updates are huge files that require a large amount of free space on your computer and take hours to upload and install. If you don't want to bother then buy a unit without lifetime maps and just replace it when the maps get old. At today's low prices that makes sense for many users.

Lifetime Traffic: Free lifetime traffic services, usually in return for displaying ads on the screen.

Loadable Maps: Almost all mapping trail GPS receivers and street GPS units allow you to add maps yourself. If you plan to use the unit outside the coverage area supplied with the receiver, make certain you can add maps. Normally, the add-on maps must be bought from the GPS manufacturer.

Motorcycle Features: Street GPS receivers that are designed for motorcycle use are waterproof to the IPX7 standard, resistant to ultraviolet (UV) light, and have special touch screens designed for use with gloves. In addition, they usually have Bluetooth so cell phone calls can be made though the audio system in your helmet. POIs can be called by selecting them from the screen. Some units have optional XM satellite radio and weather.

MP3 Player: This feature lets you store and play music.

Paperless Geocaching: This feature allows you to save notes and clues with the geocache location in the GPS receiver so you don't have to carry printed notes.

Pedestrian Navigation: A street GPS feature designed to guide you around a city on foot.

Photo Navigation: This feature lets you navigate directly to a geotagged photo stored in the receiver. A geotagged photo contains the location where the image was taken.

Picture Viewer: Lets you store and display photos. Some trail receivers also have cameras.

POI: Point-of-Interest. These are locations of places saved in a street GPS's memory, including businesses and public facilities. All street GPS receivers have databases of thousands or millions of POIs. This feature means you can locate a place by name or category rather than having to know the street address.

Powered Mount: The power/USB cable goes to the mount instead of the GPS receiver, so you don't have to connect the cable every time you mount the GPS unit.

Preloaded Maps: These maps are loaded into the unit at the factory and give coverage of a specific area at much more detail than the basemap. Trail units typically have topographic maps at a scale of 1:100,000 or better. Street GPS receivers typically have street and road maps covering a country or a region, such as the United States, North America, or Europe.

Profiles: Stores configurations for activities such as hiking, geocaching, cycling, driving, and others, saving you the trouble of changing many settings when switching uses.

QWERTY or **ABC Keyboard:** Lets you choose the layout of the virtual keyboard on the touchscreen.

Raster Maps: Maps created by scanning printed maps. For example, raster USGS 7.5-minute series topographic maps are the most detailed and accurate maps of US terrain available, but man-made features such as roads and trails are not always up to date.

Route: Routes are made up of two or more waypoints that describe a route of travel and can be saved in the GPS receiver with a descriptive name. All trail GPS receivers allow you to store multiple routes, as do some street GPS units.

Route Avoidance: Allows you to set a street GPS receiver to avoid toll roads, highways, and other undesirable routes.

Route Setup: Enables a street GPS to calculate routes by the least time, shortest distance, or off road.

Saved Geocaches: In the GPS receiver, a geocache is a waypoint with special geocaching features such as marking the cache as found and the ability to take notes.

Smartphone Link: Links to selected smartphones and uses their Internet connection to obtain real-time traffic information and other updates.

Smart Traffic: This street GPS feature uses historic traffic information such as average speeds during rush hour periods to adjust travel times.

Speed Limit Display: Shows the posted speed limit along major roads and may also warn you if you exceed the limit. Temporary speed limits such as construction zones are typically not shown.

Spoken Street Names: In addition to voice prompts, many street GPS receivers also speak the street names, which completely eliminates the need to look at the screen during critical phases of driving.

SPOT: SPOT capability allows you to transmit messages containing your GPS location through the SPOT satellite service via a paid subscription. Messages include SOS, OK, and custom messages. Friends also can track your progress on Google Maps.

Sun and Moon Data: Many trail GPS receivers can display the times of sunrise, sunset, moonrise, and moonset for any location, which is useful for backcountry trip planning.

Tides: This feature shows tide graphs for tide stations and is essential for coastal boaters and sea kayakers.

Touchscreen: All street GPS receivers and some trail units have touch-activated screens. They are best for use in-vehicle and for mild hiking conditions. Most touchscreen trail units will not work when you're wearing gloves or when the unit is protected inside a waterproof bag.

Track Log: Trail GPS receivers can be set to automatically store waypoints as you travel, creating a track log that can be saved and also used to backtrack your route.

Traffic: This street GPS feature lets you see real-time traffic data, such as congestion and accidents. May require a monthly or annual fee.

Trucking Features: Street GPS receivers optimized for trucking and RV use. They usually have larger screens, louder speakers, and truck-specific speed limits, routing and POIs. RV drivers can set vehicle profiles so that routes are calculated that meet height, width, and weight limits. Data logging lets you track hours and fuel use.

User Route Prediction: Allows a street GPS to take into account user preferences when computing a route to the chosen destination.

Vector Maps: Digital maps created on a computer or GPS screen from mapping data. Topographic vector maps are not as accurate as USGS topo maps in depicting terrain features, but trails, roads, and other man-made features are often more up to date.

Voice-Activated Navigation: Allows you to give spoken commands to a street GPS receiver.

Voice Prompts: Most street GPS receivers use a small built-in speaker to give voice driving directions. This feature is essential to avoid driver distraction caused by looking at the GPS screen.

WAAS: The Wide Area Augmentation System is a differential GPS (DGPS) system run by the Federal Aviation Administration to enhance GPS accuracy to one to three meters for air navigation. It uses geosynchronous satellites to send correction signals to the GPS receiver. Nearly all trail GPS receivers have WAAS.

Waterproof Standards: IPX7 is the common standard for GPS receivers, meaning the unit can be submerged in one meter of water for up to 30 minutes. Trail, motorcycle, bicycling, and boating GPS receivers should be waterproof.

Waypoint: A physical location described by coordinates and labeled with a name, also called a "location" or a "favorite." All GPS navigation takes place between waypoints saved in the receiver.

Wireless Data Sharing: This feature lets you share GPS data such as waypoints with another compatible GPS unit.

XM Compatible: Capable of receiving XM Satellite Radio and weather maps with an optional subscription.

Index

About the Author

Bruce Grubbs is an avid hiker, mountain biker, paddler, and cross-country skier who has been exploring the American West for several decades. He has used high-technology gear in the backcountry in his work as a professional pilot, an amateur radio operator, and a mountain rescue team member. Bruce holds Airline Transport Pilot and Instrument Flight Instructor certificates. He lives in Flagstaff, Arizona, and is the author of more than thirty-five books.

Other books by Bruce:

Backpacker Magazine's Using a GPS

Best Easy Day Hikes Flagstaff, 2nd

Best Easy Day Hikes Sedona, 2nd

Desert Hiking Tips

Grand Canyon National Park Pocket Guide

Hiking Arizona, 3rd

Hiking Nevada, 2nd

Hiking Northern Arizona, 3rd

Mountain Biking Phoenix

Mountain Biking St. George and Cedar City

For more information, visit Bruce's website at brucegrubbs.com